# Beyond Trail's End

Dorothy Baxter Arquette
and
Judy Arquette Brassard

iUniverse, Inc.
Bloomington

iUniverse books may be ordered through booksellers or by contacting:

iUniverse
1663 Liberty Drive
Bloomington, IN 47403
www.iuniverse.com
1-800-Authors (1-800-288-4677)

ISBN: 978-1-4620-1627-3 (pbk)
ISBN: 978-1-4620-1628-0 (cloth)
ISBN: 978-1-4620-1629-7 (ebk)

Printed in the United States of America

iUniverse rev. date: 4/29/2011

In
Memory Of
Delbert E. Baxter
1886 - 1986

# Acknowledgments

We would like to express our deep appreciation to Ruth Roach, our dear sister and aunt for her input, memories and encouragement.

Also to children and siblings, Polly, Johnnie, and Denis, and to all other family members who contributed in one way or another.

A special thank you to the members of the Stearns family who so generously supplied pictures and stories, the grandchildren of Gaylord and Bessie: Barbara Miller, Mary Audrey Marvin, and to Susan Zimmer (a great-granddaughter) for answering our first inquiries about Gaylord and Bessie's descendents.

To Fran Panico for her skills and hours of work proofreading helping to make this book a reality.

To Joan Eurto for sharing her expertise and thoughtful input.

And, thank you to all of you out there in the web world who answered our inquiries about Peace River country.

# Preface

Based on his true life experiences we retell the story of Delbert Baxter's young life and try to paint a picture of what his world was like during the early twentieth century in the United States and the Canadian west.

We have tried to keep the stories as true as possible. Many of the characters in this book were people that Del talked about, although the names may not be accurate. Most of the places he described well. Some places required a little research. Whenever he was asked where he lived on his trap line, he would simply reply; "In Peace River country, east of the Pine, not far from a trading post where the East and West Pine Rivers meet."

Our purpose for writing this book is not only to keep the stories alive for Del's future generations but also for readers everywhere to enjoy the same stories that we enjoyed listening to all our years of growing up.

# Chapter 1
## LEAVING HOME

Delbert E Baxter

The exact date that Delbert Baxter left home and headed for the west is unclear. In all the stories he was to tell his family in his later years, he never once declared an exact date of his departure. For the sake of being in the proximity, we will call it 1911, probably in the late spring or early summer. We do know before he left he had been married briefly and the marriage sadly ended in divorce. He was young, very young and filled with stubborn pride. The bitterness, hurt and anger of a divorce was difficult to bear. His disillusionment came before he had experienced much of what life had to offer. Burying his disappointment deep inside, he left the only world he had ever known behind him.

Del was born on December 18, 1886 on a farm located in the St. Lawrence River Valley in Northern New York. He was one of eight children, six sons and two daughters born to Laban and Alice Corey Baxter.

The Baxters were a hearty sort with a natural instinct for fitness and survival, descendents of American colonists who endured many hardships while clearing and settling the land that they fought for in the Revolutionary War. Being one of the first founding families in St. Lawrence County, their lives were filled with hard work. They were farmers, carpenters and loggers with a logging camp in the Adirondacks. The yearning to seek a new land to explore and settle was buried deep within Delbert's roots. The ancient paths of his ancestors were calling him, urging him to go.

With his few possessions and a one-way ticket, he boarded a train and rode as far west as the train could take him. Getting off at the end of the line, he began a journey taking him beyond the end of the trail.

# Chapter 2
## DETROIT

Del watched the changing countryside pass by as he looked out the window of the train. The open fields and often-thick forests began to disappear as a large lake loomed ahead. Following the lakeside, the train moved on, passing a large shipping yard with ships of all sizes. Freighters, cruise ships, fishing boats and tug boats were strung out for miles. A countless number of men were working about the massive docks loading and unloading cargo. Beyond the shipping yard was a congestion of large, unsightly buildings and factories. Taking a sudden turn away from the water, an enormous railroad switchyard came into view. Trains were parked everywhere on side rails running parallel to each other. Waiting freight cars, locomotives, and old passenger cars sat unused and motionless. Others were huffing, puffing with whistles blowing and steam spewing out like billowing clouds, moving around and out in all directions.

A loud whistle began to blow mercilessly strong and long as the engine slowed to a stop. They had entered the city of Detroit, Michigan, the last stop for this part of Del's trip.

Anticipation, excitement and a small fear washed over him. In all of his 25 years, he had never been to a city this large. Some friends from Massena, the Sheehan family, had moved here a few years ago. He had planned to look them up and get some bearings on where to travel next.

Stepping off the train onto the depot boardwalk, Del looked around taking in the smell, noise and chaos of the large railroad station. The yard was filled with horse drawn carriages and a few motorcars. People were everywhere moving at a quick pace and workers were shouting and running about. Everyone was in a hurry.

He followed the other passengers and found his way to claim his luggage. Entering the station house, he found a clerk and showed him the Sheehan's address printed neatly on a small piece of paper he had taken out of his shirt

3

pocket. The clerk looked Del over conspicuously and somehow knew this young man was not a city boy. With a friendly smile, he pulled out a map of the city and together they soon found the street. It would be a good hike, the clerk told him. The best thing to do would be to catch a ride on the trolley car going up Woodward and get off at the corner of Third Street North. From there it would be an easy walk of two blocks.

Outside the station house the clerk pointed out where to catch the trolley. Shaking Del's hand he wished him luck. With renewed assurance and confidence, Del picked up his baggage and headed out.

A short time later, he stood in front of a small wood frame home that looked much the same as every other house on the street. It was, however, marked with the house number written on the paper he was still holding in his hand. After knocking on the door, it opened and he was met with a squeal of delight. He was quickly ushered in, for they had been expecting him and sure were happy to see a face from home. They had received his letter and had been eagerly waiting.

Del stayed with the Sheehans for a week. They showed him around their new city and hoped he would decide to find work and stay there. Detroit was a growing industrial town and work could be found in almost any of the many factories.

The more Del saw the more he knew it was not the place for him. About his third day there, he confided this to his friend as they shared a cold drink on the front porch. The warm, humid evening clung to his skin, clammy and sticky. A breath of air hardly stirred at all. The sounds of the neighborhood children running and playing, people shouting at each other and at their horses as they rode along in the buggies, and the occasional automobile sputtering by, left the surroundings anything but quiet. He could never live here without going plum crazy. Nope, farming was his way of life and the country was the only place he could live.

"I need to see the stars spread across the night sky with sounds of the crickets and frogs coming to life being the only noise. I need to hear a soft wind rushing through the pines making them whisper. I miss seeing a summer sun-rise breaking over the tree tops beyond a meadow flowing with tall green grass and cattle grazing close to a small brook." The more he talked the more he began to become homesick for his little farm far away. He was restless and he wanted to see more of the country.

There was lots of talk about work in the wheat fields out west. Farms in the west were huge. Wheat fields covered thousands of acres and harvesting time was getting close. Ads calling for men to work the fields filled the local newspaper. Choosing one in the mid-west, he decided that was as good a place as any to start. There were also government ads describing lands to be granted for homesteading. Del read with curiosity and the idea grew in his mind.

# *Chapter 3*
## CHICAGO

Detroit faded out of sight as the early morning train carried Del on his journey farther west. Chicago would soon be coming up ahead, but as it would happen, it would take a long time to get there.

Sometimes destiny plays a part in our lives and will put us in just the right place at just the right time. Although Del certainly made a clear decision to board this train on this particular day, good ole fate may well have played a hand in his decision. Before the day was over, a certain railroad crew chief, along with several workers, were sure that God himself had sent Del there.

Much earlier that day, just ahead of them, a train coming into Chicago's switchyard had derailed. With no way of rerouting around the accident, Del's train could do nothing but sit idly by and wait. Other passengers were getting off the train, so Del decided to follow and see what was going on up ahead.

Luckily no one was seriously injured, for it was not a large wreck. The tracks were torn up badly and pieces of rail had been strewn about with some of them standing on end. It would take several hours for railroad workers to clear up the wreckage and repair the tracks. The damaged cars had already been moved off the site. The men where now desperately trying to clear the broken tracks so they could lay down new ones. One large rail was driven deep into the ground right in the middle of the railroad bed. The crew worked in vain to pull it out. Someone came up with the idea to back up the engine as close as possible and wrap a chain around the end of the rail that protruded from the ground. They attached the other end of the chain to the engine. However, as soon as the engine moved ahead, it would pull the chain right off the rail and not move it a bit.

Del stood with the crowd of onlookers and watched. Nothing seemed to work and the men were getting more and more frustrated. Looking over the work crew, Del walked up to the guy who appeared to be in charge and asked if he could help. He told the crew chief that he had been watching and thought he knew what they were doing wrong. With his experience in logging back home in the Adirondacks, he had come across similar situations.

"I think I can help you out here," Del offered, "If you will let me put a hand to it, I can show you what to do. I can try to put a hitch on the chain that should hold."

The man looked at him doubtfully. He felt nearly defeated and here stood this young man confident that he knew what to do. The crew had worked for hours and the clock was ticking away. It was imperative that they get this mess cleaned up. He had to get this train running as soon as possible. All the broken rails had to be removed before they could finish the repair work and they had been stuck on this one damn rail for a long time. He told him to go ahead and try; right about now they would try anything.

Del walked over and told the engineer to back up a little bit and give the chain some slack. Taking the chain in hand, he wrapped it around the end of the rail in what he called a half hitch. He then instructed the engineer to tighten it up, but "to go slow". The engine started to move ahead...... very slowly. The chain became tight and started to pull on the rail. Giving it just a little more power, the rail came right up and out of the ground. A loud shout was heard as the crowd of on-lookers all cheered and praised Del. The crew chief walked over and shook his hand, pumping his arm up and down. He couldn't thank him enough. This young man had saved the day!

# Chapter 4
## WORKING THE WHEAT FIELDS

Del's train ride ended in a small mid-western town in the middle of prairie land, the breadbasket of our country. Rolling fields of grass flowed about as far as the eye could see. In the far off distance, here and there a windmill stood near a farmhouse and barn. The town itself didn't seem much more than a wide spot in the road, a dusty crossroad with several buildings. The mid-summer sun beat mercilessly, strong and hot. It must be 90 degrees in the shade, Del thought. How different this was from the weather in northern New York.

The local mercantile served as a general store, post office, and feed store. It seemed to be a likely place to get information. Inquiring within, he found where he could get a room at a boarding house down the street and the best place to buy a horse or two. The harvesters would be out working the wheat fields at local farms. If he was to get hired he needed to travel out there and find them. He found a good enough saddle horse and bought him for a reasonable sum. He also came across a young, mean-looking creature nobody else wanted that would make a fine packhorse. Del thought with a little bit of training, he would do okay.

The next morning, Del worked with his new horses getting them ready for his ride out to the farms. Much to his dismay, the scruffy little packhorse would have nothing to do with being loaded down with supplies and gear. The little horse made an awful fuss, bucking and kicking and it even tried to bite Del. Del didn't have much patience for this type of behavior, but he wasn't going to give up. He decided the best way to handle the situation was to saddle up the critter and ride him until he was broke in. After some work, he managed to get into the saddle and away they went.

The horse kicked and bucked and managed to get the bit in his teeth so that he couldn't be controlled. He ran and ran for miles, it seemed like, and it was. About the time the horse began to tire they had came close to one of the local farms. Del got him stopped when he saw a farmer in a nearby field. The farmer was glad to give him some water for the tired out animal but Del was careful not to let him drink too much. After the disappointment of finding out that the harvesters had been there and had already moved north, he started out again.

"Well I guess that was a good workout," Del said out loud more to himself than to the horse. "I think you will do all right," he chuckled. "Buck, that's a good name for you. Come on Buck, let's head back for town."

When he got back to town, he watered both the horses and fed them a little grain in their nosebags. It was getting late in the day, so he decided to get something to eat at the diner before he headed out. This time he managed to get Buck loaded up and together, with Del riding the saddle horse, they rode out onto the prairie.

It had been a long time since Del had been able to enjoy the great outdoors. This is what he had been waiting for, to ride the open prairie and live under the clear open sky. It was a strange land, almost like another world, so different and exciting to explore. Before darkness fell, Del had found a small stream and followed it back away from the road a short disstance where there was plenty of grass and water from the stream for the horses. He made camp for the night, but didn't start his fire. Having eaten in town, he didn't need the campfire to cook his supper but he knew he would need it for coffee and breakfast in the morning. He fixed up some kindling and laid some small sticks on it so it would be ready for early morning. The fresh night air was soothing and the stars overhead shone brightly as he fixed up a bed with his canvas and some blankets.

Sometime in the middle of the night, Del awoke from a sound sleep. Something was out there in the darkness of the night. Opening his eyes, he listened carefully without making a move. Some critter was making the strangest noise he had ever heard. It sounded like a squawk, such as what a big bird might make. But what big bird would be out there flying around in the middle of the night? The squawk kept moving, going around and around as if circling him. Jumping out of his blankets, he wasn't long in starting the fire that he had laid for his breakfast. Del sat up the rest of the night keeping the fire going and watching for whatever wild animal was out there after him.

When morning finally arrived, there was nothing to be seen. He was alone by tall grasses and the stream flowing all around. It was some time later before he learned that this strange sound belonged to nothing more fierce than a prairie hen!

# Chapter 5
## HARVESTING

Del got hired on with the harvesters and soon fit right in with the many young men. Some worked the shocks (standing up bundles of wheat into large bunches) and others worked with the reapers and threshing machines. Working with his two older brothers back home on a threshing machine gave him the advantage of experience. The days were long and hot as Del brought in wagons from the fields and unloaded the crop into the machine. Sometimes he and the other fellows bringing in the wheat would get far ahead of the threshers and would have to unload their grain, piling up big stacks. The crew usually would not stop work for the night until just about dusk.

Even after working hard all day, Del could not sit without anything to do and would often work with his horses. His fondness for working with horses paid off when, after hours of training, they were soon pulling a wagon as a team. He was then able to use them to help draw the wagons full of wheat in from the fields.

Throughout the harvesting, he ended up working many jobs. The thresher was a monster of a machine powered by a steam engine with big boilers heated by coal. It took four horses to draw the machine from one wheat field to another. Along with the thresher, the wagons drawing in the grain and a large reaper were also pulled by at least four horses. This made many horses to care for, a job Del enjoyed the most.

He soon found another job when the crew discovered his talent for cooking: chief camp cook. Back east on the little home farm, Del's mother taught her children to be helpful and independent in many ways. The boys, right along with the girls, had been taught how to cook, sew and even knit mittens. The appreciation for these practical tasks would be felt over and over throughout his long life.

Many times the field workers would eat their meals at the farm on which they were working. The farmer's wife cooked large hearty meals and served them on tables set up outside. The crew had a chuck wagon loaded with supplies for their early morning breakfast and the occasional times when no meals were supplied for them. The day finally came when it was Del's turn to cook for the crew's supper. He willingly took to this project. He found some beans soaking in a big kettle. After getting a fire going, he put them on to cook. This would take awhile, so while he was waiting he looked over the rest of the supplies and found some flour, sugar, meat and dried apples. To his surprise, there in the wagon was a nice Dutch oven (a covered dish for baking that could be set into the coals of the camp fire). He had everything needed to cook a feast. Keeping the fire going under the beans, he prepared to bake a pie with the dried apples, then effortlessly made some biscuits to go with the beans and fried meat. It wasn't long before the men came in from the field. They all announced that something sure smelled good and could not believe their eyes when they saw the apple pie. After the delicious supper, they decided Del should be made the permanent cook. He talked his way out of being the head cook but would often take over when asked. When the opportunity presented itself, he would buy a few chickens from one of the farmers and surprise the whole crew with chicken and dumplings.

The summer passed quickly and fall arrived. The harvesting was finished and the long cold harsh winter was close at hand. A farmer and his wife wanted to go back east to escape the cold of the prairie and asked Del to stay at their place to watch over the homestead. Having nowhere else to go, Del quickly agreed. The work was not hard; there were just a few milk cows, some chickens and horses to look after. The family of homesteaders had worked hard to settle the land and build their home.

It was a nice and comfy place, but it was very isolated with the nearest neighbor several miles away. To fill up his time, and when the weather permitted, Del would often go hunting. The men on the harvesting crew had taught him a few tricks for hunting on the prairie. Using a long piece of prairie grass, he would place it between his two hands and blow hard, making a squealing noise. The noise sounded a lot like what a rabbit would make, and if a fox or coyote was near enough, it would follow the sound to investigate. With his rifle handy, Del would take the opportunity to shoot the unsuspecting animal and skin it for its fur.

The house was very quiet and unsettling living in it by himself. In the home was an old Edison phonograph that played cylinder records. Thinking it would be nice to play some music, Del put on a cylinder and cranked it up, but it didn't work. He decided to take the phonograph apart and see what was wrong with it. It had a broken spring. Since there were many daylight hours in which he had no chores, he managed to fix the spring and put the machine back together. At last, he could play some music for his relaxation and enjoyment. He wound up the crank and music began to play.

The song it played was so familiar. The soft music filled the empty silence of the room bringing a fond memory to his mind. Del suddenly thought about home and could picture his mother playing her piano as the whole family stood around her, singing this same song. An overwhelming lonesomeness washed over him. He had never longed for the sight of his parents and home the way he did now. Taking the cylinder record off the machine, he closed the cover and never played it again.

# Chapter 6
## Moving North

And so the winter passed. Del made a few trips into town to buy supplies and visit with some of the locals. The long evenings were filled with working on projects, whittling little pieces of wood into some kind of useful tool, or knitting heavy warm socks and mittens for himself. They were sure useful while working outside during the extremely cold winter days, carrying wood and shoveling snow. Again, he would think about his mother sitting by his side, teaching him to knit and sew.

Winter was barely hanging on as the days began to get longer and warmer. Spring was moving in early; the owners would be returning.

During his stay at the farm, he had found an old broken-down wagon out behind the barn. It had been in pretty bad shape, but by the time Del was finished with it, it was as good as new. The rancher let Del buy it for a fair price after all the work he had put into it. Now that he owned a wagon to hold his belongings and two horses to pull it, he was ready to continue on his journey.

After lots of thought on what his next endeavor would be, he decided to try his hand at homesteading. The idea of being granted land to call his own, just for the price of working it into farmland, intrigued him. One hundred and sixty acres was not near as big as his father's farm back home, but it was a nice place to start. With confidence in his own ability and know-how, he dreamed of what he could do. He wanted to meet the challenge of succeeding with a farm on the prairie.

By this time, all of the land available for homesteading in the States had been allotted. The only homesteads available now were in the plains of the Canadian provinces. "Well, why not Canada?" Del thought to himself. He had no boundaries on his travels or limits on his time to worry about. By following the harvesting, he had already worked his way far north. Canada was not that far away. His next venture had been decided; Del would soon make Alberta, Canada his home.

Along the way, he made a crude covering for his wagon. This made adequate shelter for him and his possessions from the intense searing sun and the occasional heavy spring rain. Keeping to the trails by day, he would camp out at night and do a little bit of hunting and trapping. The land was abundant with deer, elk and rabbit. The furs would be saved for the trading post and a good prairie rabbit always tasted good after being cooked over the campfire.

Del traveled many miles in a day but it still took him several days to cross the border. When he finally did, he discovered he had been in Saskatchewan for awhile before he even knew it. Following the telegraph wires was a traveler's guide along the countryside of the wide-open prairie. The path led him to a little town called Alsask, which proved to be a good stopping place. Alsask was the end of the line for the railroad and an interesting little settlement just east of the Alberta border, barely into Saskatchewan. Because of this, its name was derived from the combination of the two provinces of Alberta and Saskatchewan. Homesteads in this part of Saskatchewan were no longer available, but a short ride into Alberta proved successful.

Twenty-five miles west of Alsask, in the midst of a prairie terrain, a small community lay along the eastern part of Alberta. Oyen existed as a mere crossroads on a trail which led east to west from Calgary to Saskatoon, southeast of Edmonton and north of Medicine Hat. Del traveled twenty miles north of this little town and settled there.

A land management office was found to take care of signing up for a homestead. A section of land was 600 acres, but each homesteader was allowed 160 acres. A government man took Del out to look over his section, which made him a little bit more reassured. Del said he had never bought a "pig in a poke" before and needed to see just what it was he would be taking over.

The earth was covered in tall grasses glowing golden under the prairie sun. A small number of cottonwood trees grew near a small stream that ran along the edge of the land. The song and ceaseless hum of living creatures along with the murmur of the wind blowing across the terrain welcomed him. Here was a land where gardens and crops could grow, horses, oxen, cows and chickens could thrive. Here was a place to call home.

# *Chapter 7*
## BUILDING A HOMESTEAD

Most of the homesteaders on the prairie had endured many hardships during their journey from great distances to claim their land. Men, women and children took up the challenge to become pioneers in their own right by settling a wilderness and making homes and communities where only the buffalo, elk and other wild species had survived before them. They came with all of their belongings loaded onto wagons pulled by oxen or horses over nothing more than rough trails. The wagons would often lurch down steep gullies and flounder across swollen streams, moving slowly back up steep grades under the grueling hot sun day after day. It was backbreaking and heartbreaking, but still they pushed on to make a new life for themselves on land they could call their own.

Many came from the east, Ontario and Quebec; others from the United States. Many were foreigners coming from all over the world such as Germany, Poland, Holland, and Scotland. The immigrants sailed on ships from the old countries into Quebec and from there traveled west by train to the town closest to their land grant. After buying wagons and oxen or horses to carry all of their belongings, the rest of their trip would be slow, traveling about 20 miles in a day.

As the people settled their land, they encouraged each other by working together. This community spirit eased the endurance of many difficult times, seemingly to lessen the many day-to-day hardships.

Homes were built on the closest corner of each 160-acre lot to border their neighbors. This way, although they were still quite isolated, the distance from each other was not too great. You could find a home usually within a mile or two.

There was a lack of trees for logs to build homes and the settlers would have to travel great distances to buy lumber shipped in from other areas of the country by train. Because of this, many of the homes were temporary sod houses with flat roofs, created out of the natural soil and built into the hillside. The roofs were built with twigs, branches and bushes and covered with more chunks of turf. Although the heavy rains would often leak through, it was the quickest and easiest way to make a shelter for a family.

Having established his claim, Del was now in Oyen buying supplies, tools and food. The store was a general meeting place for many of the folks in the area, especially on mail day, as the mail would arrive once a week. People would make the drive into town to collect their mail and purchase needed supplies for home. Many were friendly and eager to welcome Del to the area. One particular man, who appeared to be about 10 years older, struck up a conversation. Del was hungry for conversation having traveled so far alone. The man had a warm smile and a firm handshake and Del took an instant liking to him. He gave Del good advice on what supplies he would need and how to go about beginning to work the land to prove his claim. His name was Stearns, Gaylord Stearns, and he lived not far out of town with his wife, Bessie, and five children. Before long Gaylord had Del talked into going out to his homestead with him to meet the family and have a good home cooked meal. As fate would have it; Del and Gaylord would become very close life long friends.

The Stearns family had come from the States not too long before. Their wood frame house was completed and Gaylord had done some plowing getting ready to put in a garden and some crops. Bessie and the children, Harry, Ralph, Grace, Fred and Gaylord, welcomed Del warmly, always happy to have company and especially someone new from the States. Over a well-appreciated hot meal, Del learned that Gaylord had been born in North Dakota while Bessie was from Iowa. Their first son, Harry, was born in North Dakota and they later moved to Hillyard, Washington near Spokane. Their next two children, Ralph and Grace, were born there. Bessie had traveled home to Iowa for the birth of their fourth child, Fred, and baby Gaylord was born right here in Alberta.

"When did you come out here?" Del asked.

[1]"We settled here in 1910." Bessie replied. "Oyen wasn't here then. Alsask was thirty miles away and it was our only town where we could go for supplies and everything for sometime. The settlers were very scarce at that time. We were lucky as to where we picked our land as we found a neighbor, Mr. Michael. He brought a new bride out the same day that I and the children

---

1    Story by Bessie Stearns, Life on The Alberta Prairie submitted with permission from the Stearns family

came out to our new home on our prairie land. All we could see was buffalo grass, a few alkali ponds and a couple of homesteader shacks. We found our new neighbors to be very kind and good neighbors.

I came here after Gaylord. He came first with some other men and took a few weeks to locate our land. It was quite an experience for me, traveling here. I came out to Alsask by rail from Winnipeg on a settlers' train. It was very crowded with families with little children coming to different places in Saskatchewan and Alberta. It was a long trip, and I had an eight month old baby and three other small children. One or two of the cars jumped the track and we were held up for eight or ten hours. It was hard for us young mothers with babies and small children and no place to buy food or milk. But, to my surprise, the men in the cars made a bigger fuss about the delay than the children did."

# Chapter 8
## FAIR ACRES

Del listened carefully to the sounds of early morning. Something had awakened him and it wasn't even daylight yet. There it was again, a soft hoot-hoot of an owl. The great horned owl had been hanging around his campsite for the last few nights, most likely in the trees close to the creek. He was awake now, so he might as well get up and start his day. He climbed out of his little covered wagon and started to build a campfire for his coffee and breakfast. Filling his coffee pot from the water barrel, he threw some coffee grounds into it and set it on top of the grate covering the small fire. Sitting before the fire waiting for the coffee to brew, he watched his animals stirring, mere shadows in the haze of pre-dawn. Quietly they moved about chewing on the abundant prairie grass. Two oxen shared the corralled meadow with his two horses. He had been lucky enough to buy the oxen from an old homesteader who was selling out and moving back to Ontario. The oxen were big, slow, clumsy critters, but in many ways they worked well; you just had to know how to handle them. The oxen were needed for the hard heavy work of a farm on the prairie. They could pull heavy loads and go farther and work longer than horses.

Using his little covered wagon to camp in was working out okay for now. Sometimes, on really hot nights, he would simply roll out a blanket on the ground and use the stars as a roof over his head. A portion of his land was worked up and ready to sow. The little garden was already planted. The lumber to build his wood frame house was being shipped by train from Edmonton to Alsask and should arrive in about two more days. A plain one level house with a loft would do nicely here. The Soddy's were interesting little dwellings, but sure didn't look comfy to him. Besides, with his skill and know-how, he would have a good solid home built in no time.

The sun began to peak across the horizon as Del was sipping his coffee.

Sunrise on the prairie is a sight. Rising above the gently rolling hills, the sun casting rays of light across soft flowing grasses was almost like being at sea with waves rising and falling. The wise old owl was no longer around but a small falcon swooped nearby. He glided low, his wings spread wide, searching for field mice, rabbits or any little rodent taking shelter along the creek side. The chorus of a few bobolinks began to chirp. Morning had arrived.

As the morning light moved in, Del reached in his pocket and pulled out an envelope. The nice long letter from mother had arrived yesterday at the store in Oyen addressed to Delbert Baxter, Fair Acres, Oyen, Alberta, Canada. Del felt a surge of pride reading the name of his farm, Fair Acres. After quickly reading it he put it away. Now while soaking up the soft morning breeze, he leisurely opened the treasured letter and read each word more carefully. Mother wrote nice letters and her words painted a picture of home and its activities.

*My Dear Son,*

*I think of you everyday and wonder how you are doing and what you are doing, so far away out there in that wild land.*

*Pa and the boys have been putting in hay and between field work and cutting wood have been helping Ozzie out at his new farm. Ozzie and Alice bought the Harry Smith farm over in Knapps Station. It is a nice place sitting right on the edge of the brook. Ozzie is clearing part of the land to set up a sawmill. He just left here a little while ago; he came over to do some harness work in Pa's black-smith shop. Emery and Clint have been working hard with him and even Homer can help out some now at eleven years old. He is pretty much their go-getter.*

*Your Pa never ceases to amaze me with the crazy ideas he comes up with and is still spending his good money on his animals. He sent away to Vermont for another fox hound and this time paid $60 for it. And I thought buying the first one at $40 was bad. When the dog arrived he brought it home still in the crate. One of the boys opened the door before Pa could get to him. The $60 hound ran off and has never been seen again.*

*A few weeks ago he made a trip all the way to Ohio and bought a Jackass for $600 and had him crated by railroad to Massena. He plans to mate him with some of our mares and raise mules to sell.*

*He does have a nice new pair of bays now and he is so proud of them. He loves to show them off every chance he gets and will challenge a race with anyone who will give him the satisfaction of trying.*

*Old Flossie is getting really old but she will still go out with Homer on her back and round up the cows. I remember when Clint & Emery where so little, Ozzie would put one of them on Flossie and she would mozzie on down the pasture to bring up the cows without them guiding her at all. She would always be careful going under trees so as not to knock them off. Flossie always preferred Clint, although she would go with Emery. But, if the two little boys stood in front of her together, she would always nudge Clint with her nose. Now Clint is sixteen and Emery is almost eighteen. They can run down the pasture to get the cows faster than that poor old horse can go.*

*Pa, Emery and Clint are making plans to come out to visit you next year. You should be pretty well settled by then. They are so curious about the land you have and what the western countryside is like. I have to admit I would like to see it myself, but will have to rely on their memories. It is a long way off yet anyway.*

*I better close now. The boys will be in from the barn soon, looking for their supper. You take care of yourself and stay healthy and strong. Please write to us soon and keep us informed on how you are doing.*

*Love from all, Mother*


Folding up the letter Del tucked it away in a small wooden box inside the wagon. Today was Sunday and Del had decided that after washing up and shaving he would gather up all of his clothes and bedding and do a washing. He had drawn some water from the creek and had it heating in the kettle sitting on the campfire for this purpose. He pulled out his washtub and scrub board from under the wagon where they had been stored.

After reading mother's letter, she was much on his mind. While scrubbing his clothes his mind wandered, thinking back to a time long ago.

It was wash day and Del was helping mother carry the bundle of laundry down to the river bank across from their home. The Raquette was not a big river but it was very large compared to the little creek he had here. Pa, Ozzie and Herb were going deer hunting. They went down to the river and crossed in a rowboat to the big woods. Del had wanted to go with them but Pa said he was needed here to help his mother. At 10 years old he sure felt left out, but someone had to build the fire and get water in the kettle for mother to wash the clothes. He ran around looking for twigs and sticks to keep the fire burning.

The younger kids played around the riverside. Luella was only seven and too little to help mother very much; Emery was two years old and Clint was just a newborn.

The river here was very swift as it was just below big rapids. The banks went almost straight down; if you fell in, it was almost impossible to climb out. Del watched out for Emery and Luella playing along the bank throwing stones in the water as he chopped up sticks with a small ax. Mother boiled the clothes in the big iron kettle with lye soap then pulled them out with a forked stick that she kept for that purpose. She then dropped them into a tub of cold water.

They had been working at this for some time when Del saw something moving across the river. A big buck was running hard, probably scared up by the hunters. His path came to the river's edge downstream near the rapids. The driven animal plunged into the water and began to swim for the other shore, but the current was so strong it carried the deer down stream. The deer soon tired of the swift water and tried to come ashore, but the bank was too steep for him to get a foothold to climb out. As the large animal struggled to get on land, Mother dropped her washing, picked up Del's ax and ran to the water's edge. Without hesitating, she gave that deer an awful blow in the head with the ax. Then she grabbed one of his horns and called for Del to help her. Together they pulled him up onto shore. Mother hit him again a time or two to make sure he wouldn't get up and run away. She sent Del up to the house to get the butcher knife. When he brought it back she cut the deer's throat so he would bleed out.

It was much later when Pa and the boys came home. It was time to do the evening chores. They were hungry as bears; they had no deer. Pa said they had jumped a big buck but he disappeared before anyone got a shot at him.

Del chuckled out loud as the memory worked through his mind. "That was the day," he thought, "that mother got one over on Pa."

Mother (Alice Baxter)

21

# Chapter 9
## SUNDAY DINNER

A shadow moved behind the wagon. Quick footsteps rustled in the grass. Del caught a glimpse of a red shirt out of the corner of his eye as he steeled himself for the attack. The red shirt was on him. Twisting and turning, they rolled on the ground. Del jumped up laughing and rolled the red shirt, topped with wavy sandy hair, over and pulled him to his feet. They then laughed together and slapped each other on the back.

"You have to learn to be better at that. I heard ya sneaking up on me." Del laughed as he playfully punched Harry Stearns in the arm. "Whatcha doin over here anyway?"

"Ma sent me to remind you to come to Sunday dinner. She's been cookin' all morning. The Barns family is gonna be there, too."

It had become a regular custom. Del always looked forward to Bessie Stearns' Sunday dinners, and many times, one or more of the neighbors would be there.

"I'll be there and you better be ready to play ball," Del said as he pulled out from the wagon a piece of leftover board that he had whittled, sanded and shaped into a baseball bat.

"Wow!!" is all nine year old Harry could say, handling the bat as if it were made of glass. He ran his hand up and down the smooth finish; his big eyes looked up at Del with complete admiration and a big grin spread across his small face.

"You really gonna show us how to play ball? Real baseball?"

Harry's excitement made Del's heart light and happy. Thoughts of sharing a warm Sunday afternoon with the people he had come to think of as family filled his mind.

And so, that is the way it went. Del spent Sunday afternoons with his friends and neighbors and became a real part of the community of new settlers. The social events would be shared, taking place at different homes. After dinner they would usually enjoy a good game of baseball along with horseshoes. Sometimes they would enjoy singing and dancing to music as men played their violins, guitars and mouth organs. The festivities would last well into the night.

The days of summer moved on and passed quickly. With the help of Gaylord and many of his other neighbors, Del not only built his house, but a small barn for the animals and also dug a well. Rocks that had been dug up while plowing had been saved and used to line the cellar walls for a good foundation for the house.

It took quite a while to hand-dig a well. When the hole was deep enough, Del climbed down in with a bucket. The leather handle of this bucket was tied to a rope. After he filled the bucket, Gaylord hauled it up, dumped it and sent it back down to Del. Most of the day had passed by the time water started seeping in. As soon as it did, Gaylord passed stones down in the bucket. Del packed the stones into the side of the well so the walls of dirt would not cave in or wash away. Using a ladder to climb up and down the dirt hole, they succeeded in closely fitting stones together all around to make a nice, secure water well. Placing boards over the top of the well kept it clean and safe. When water was needed, all Del had to do was drop the bucket down and pull it up with the attached rope.

Del furnished his home with a hand built table, bench and bunk bed. On this he laid a mattress covered with tick material and stuffed with prairie grass. A few shelves along the wall and one big cupboard were constructed to hold his food supplies, cooking utensils and his few dishes.

A little garden had been worked, leveled and planted with a hoe and rake. Del was rewarded with carrots, turnips, onions, and potatoes for his efforts. After digging them out of their plots in the ground, they were laid out to dry. A bin in the cellar had been put together to hold them. Covered with sand, the vegetables would be preserved for the winter.

The harvesters came to the area and Del waited his turn to have his fields reaped and thrashed. It was a good year for the grain and the harvest did well, much better than he had expected from the start. He had more than enough oats needed for his animals and was even able to sell the rest at the market. The oxen pulled the big wagon filled with grain to Alsask where the load of oats was weighed and unloaded into a railroad boxcar. The empty wagon was then weighed to determine how many pounds were in the crop. The farmers were paid for their crop by the bushel. It took a large amount of oats at 32 pounds in a bushel to earn enough to make a decent amount of money for all of their work.

Days when the regular work of the farm was finished, Del would spend a lot of time hunting. Gaylord Stearns or a few of the other neighbors would sometimes join him. Together on their horses they would travel over the prairie and rouse up a deer, prairie hen or rabbits. They all enjoyed the shared meat, and Del would keep the skins of the animals then stretch and dry them to sell to the fur trader in Oyen. The prairie wolves were a welcome hunt as the fur was much sought after.

Del had plenty of work to keep him busy and he especially enjoyed working with wood, building his house, barn and furniture. With leftover wood scraps and boards, he could plan projects to work on all winter long to share with his new friends and neighbors. By the end of the summer, Del's land was now his home.

# Chapter 10
## THE BLIZZARD

Del's first winter on the prairie would be one he would never forget. Blizzards on the prairie can move in fast and without warning, as he was soon to find out the hard way.

Summer had faded away and fall moved in silently stealing the long hot days. Each day grew shorter and the air cooler and more pleasant. The sky had been dark gray for the last few days. He hadn't seen sunshine in a week and it looked like snow was coming in any time now. Del had been doing some fall plowing in a field close to his house. He had many furrows done, working slowly up and down the field walking behind the oxen pulled plow. He was at the farther end of the field when suddenly, a cold sharp wind whipped up. As Del moved his eyes toward the dark sky, a flurry of snow pelted down upon him. The blowing snow fell so hard that it soon became blinding. The wind cut into him like ice and took his breath away without mercy. Putting his arm over his face he took big gulps of air to relieve the suffocation. Looking out across the field, all he could see was snow. It was as though a big white sheet of blowing ice had been dropped about him. Del was in the midst of a full blizzard. He could not even tell which way to go to get back to the house or barn.

Turning the oxen loose, he knew they would put their backs to the wind and keep going until they found shelter. The plowed furrows of earth went in a straight line right up to the side of his barn. If only he could pick the right direction to go. He was quite sure the barn was at the back of the plow so he started moving in that direction. With his head bent low he looked straight down staying in the deep furrow, going more by feel than sight. Fighting the cold relentless wind all the way, he stumbled and fell. Feeling around the ground with his hands, he found the lines of the freshly plowed dirt furrow and crawled on his hands and knees, using the furrow as his guide. It seemed like he was moving slowly in this direction for too long, but just about the time he began to think he must be going in the wrong direction, he bumped smack into the side of the barn. To his relief he stood hanging onto the side of the barn and moved around to the door. There he found refuge until the blizzard subsided.

He had heard stories about people being lost in a blizzard and freezing to death just a few short feet away from their homes. Now, he totally understood how this could happen. Back home there were hard snowstorms, but never had Del ever seen anything like this.

# *Chapter 11*
## THE COAL TRAIN

Within a few days, the temperature changed and brought back the warm days. The bright sun and warm air melted the snow that had fallen from the blizzard. Looking out over the field, one would never know that there had been any snowstorm at all. Del went back to working on his fall plowing and decided it was time to make a trip into Alsask to get a supply of coal for the winter. With very few trees on the prairie, coal was the major source of fuel for heating and cooking.

When he had finished the plowing, he went over to see Ben Alden. They made plans to go together to the railhead to meet the coal train when it arrived, which should be any day now.

Del's neighbor, Ben, was a widower with two young boys, nine and twelve years old. He had not been out here on his homestead very long. He had been so busy building his house and barn that he had put off getting his coal supply for the winter. The little bit he did have was dwindling fast and he had only enough left for two or three days if the weather turned cold again. Not realizing how fast the winter storms come up here on the prairie, he thought he had enough to get through until he could make the trip to buy more.

Although it worried him, Ben chose to leave his two boys home alone. They were young, but they were used to responsibility and could take care of the farm animals and each other in his absence.

Just as daylight was beginning to break through the early morning sky, Del and Ben began their two-day trip to Alsask, Saskatchewan to meet the coal train. They each had an ox driven wagon with big wooden racks to hold the coal. The oxen were monstrous animals made for work but there was no way you could make an ox move any faster than its slow heavy gait. The first day went on as they trudged through the trail. For miles and miles all they could see was the tall, thick prairie grass waving in the breeze. The sun was hot and beat down upon them as they traveled. Off in the distance they could see some cottonwood trees, brush and trundle that grew near a stream. They traveled for hours before they actually came to it. They made camp that night by the little stream. The brush and trundle was enough to build a small fire to cook their supper. The weather had become unusually warm.

They traveled all the next day and just before dark they came in sight of the railroad station. Much to their dismay, they could see wagons lined up for miles waiting for the coal train!

All they could do was get in line. They pulled up behind the other wagons and prepared to wait. The coal train had not arrived yet, but it was expected soon. Homesteaders from within a hundred miles or more were waiting and made camp near their wagons.

"It's a good thing we brought enough grub with us." said Del. "Looks like we could be here for days." Ben agreed, thinking about his boys back home "It's good it is so warm; I hope it stays this way." He hadn't planned to have to stay away this long.

The wait went on for two days before the coal train arrived. Finally someone sent up a whoop and a holler and a great cheer spread across the many camped wagons. Black smoke filled the air as the train moved in, pulling car after car filled with coal. Once the homesteaders began filling their wagons, it took another whole day before Del and Ben got their turn. For three days they had sat at the railhead. As soon as they got their wagons loaded they started for home, even though it was very late in the afternoon.

The oxen had been content to stay and eat grass where they were waiting but, so many animals had been grazing there, the grass was getting pretty scarce. Del had brought some grain along but the oxen needed their grass too.

He had learned from his Pa that you had to feed an animal if you expected it to work.

They camped just a few miles out, as it soon got dark. They made fire enough to make some coffee and warm up some flapjacks left over from breakfast. They hobbled the oxen where the grass was good, and then they rolled up in their blankets and went to sleep.

Long before dawn arrived, Del woke up shivering and freezing cold. The temperature had dropped drastically and it had started to snow. Ben was rolling out of his blanket, too. The air was so cold they could see their breath. Quickly they got ready to move out. They gave the oxen a little grain and got them hooked up to the wagons. Del and Ben chewed on some hardtack as they walked along behind their loads of coal. After a time they climbed back on their wagons and rode until the coldness was too much for them and then they would walk some more to try to warm up. Del had not thought to wear his winter shoes and socks. Walking along he would sometimes dance around a little, jumping up and down occasionally. His toes were so cold that he thought for sure they were going to fall off from frostbite. Slowly the day passed this way as they moved toward home.

It was along toward night when they saw some buildings off in the distance. It was a ways out of their way to get to it, but they decided to make the detour and maybe get shelter for the night. Darkness had started to close in by the time they reached the abandoned farm. The house turned out to be not much more than a rickety old shack. The barn was quite well built and seemed to be snug for the oxen. There was even some hay to feed them. After taking care of the oxen, Del and Ben went to investigate what was left of the ramshackle house. Wind blew through the many cracks and broken boards. There was nothing they could use to build a fire to get warm or to shelter them for the night.

The temperature was dropping even more as the night moved on. It had to be close to zero degrees or colder. They agreed the best thing to do was to go to the barn and sleep with the oxen as the body heat from the cattle would help keep the little barn warm. The barn was so small the big oxen did not leave much space. Del rolled up in his blanket near the heads of their oxen. Ben was not so willing to lay down that close to the big oxen's heads with their big horns. Having nowhere else to go, he decided to go to the back of the oxen and curl up behind their back feet with his blanket. The two men were so exhausted from their long cold day they both soon went right into a deep sleep.

It was early morning when Del woke up. He rolled out of his blanket where he had slept rather comfortably, considering. Standing up and stretching his arms, he called to Ben. "It's morning Ben. If we get hitched up now, twill be daylight by the time we get moving." No sound from Ben came back to him. Brushing the clumps of straw and dirt off his clothes, Del glanced at where Ben lay. Inside the barn it was still quite dark. Through the dimness he peered between the animals and could make out a big lump on the floor. "Ben", he called again.

"Dam. Ben said with a groan. "I can't move. Help me out!" Working his way between the animals to where Ben laid Del was taken aback at what he saw.

Ben was in quite a predicament. There he was, wrapped up tightly in his blanket; a blanket that was frozen stiff with ox manure. It was frozen so solid that Ben couldn't even move. Del quickly went out to the wagons and grabbed a shovel to chop and break up the frozen manure. Spitting and sputtering, a grateful Ben emerged from the pile of shit. His choice of sleeping space was not the wisest in the end.

Soon they were hitched up and heading toward home again. It was still a full day's journey yet and Ben was very worried about his boys. He knew they did not have enough fuel to last in this kind of weather. He couldn't imagine what they were doing to survive. His anxiety couldn't make his team of oxen move fast enough. At least it had quit snowing and they were not in danger of getting lost in a blizzard.

Daylight was fading and darkness moving in when, at last, Del and Ben could see a light coming from Ben's house. The oxen even seemed to go a little faster and soon they could smell smoke coming from the chimney. "Thank God," Ben said, "those boys have found something to burn and keep warm."

When they got close, Ben stood up in his wagon as he yelled, "Daniel, William, you in there?" In a flash the door of the cabin flew open as the two boys, wearing their heavy winter coats and boots, ran out of the house screaming. "Pa, you're home!" Daniel shouted. Will, the younger boy, just screamed continuously until he reached his father. Ben jumped from the wagon and embraced his boys as they rushed upon him. They were so glad to see their father and he was so thankful to see they were all right.

They all worked to unhook the oxen, Del's, to, and get them into the barn. Once inside the barn it became clear where the boys had gotten wood to burn to stay warm. All the petitions Ben had built for stalls and pens were gone. They had chopped them all down to burn in the stove. Luckily the men arrived when they did because the boys were just about to start on breaking up the furniture.

# Chapter 12

## RED DEER RIVER

D el stayed that night with Ben and the boys. The men were tired, but not too tired to enjoy a few games of cards after a good hot meal. Del still had a few miles to go to get home, so he headed out early in the morning. It took awhile to get the wagon unloaded and the coal stored away. Turning the oxen out in the pasture with the horses, they easily roamed looking for new grass to feed on. It was good to be home with enough coal to last all winter.

Del's contentment did not last long, however. He had heard a lot of talk about the Red Deer River area and he was eager to look it over. Within a few days, his fall work complete, he was yearning to go hunting. He took the hunting rifle down from the rack, carefully cleaned it and checked his supply of ammunition. He then made sure he packed his winter boots and clothes in preparation for his trip.

Del rode up to the Stearns' homestead leading his little packhorse loaded down with camping supplies. Bessie stood on the porch watching him ride up.

"You just get on out of here you rascal you! Yer going to run off with my man again, I can see what yer up to," she said in a teasing manner.

She gave Del a big hug as he walked toward the house. "Come in and have some coffee. Gaylord is out to the barn with the boys finishing up the chores."

Bessie really didn't mind Gaylord going off on the hunting trip. Their cold storage room was almost empty and they sure needed some fresh meat to prepare before winter set in. Gaylord and Del had earlier put up a nice size smoke house for just that purpose. Eager to hunt some big game, the two men rode out heading south.

Autumn was in full grandeur with cloudless blue skies, sharp morning air turning almost sultry by mid-afternoon. South of Oyen, about 40 miles or so, they came to the big Red Deer River (a tributary of the Saskatchewan River flowing southeast). Many of the trees and shrubs along the shoreline boasted yellow-rich hues of color mixed with shrubs of wild red rose hips. The river valley was lush with wildlife and birds of all kinds. Swift waters wildly flowed over rocks and around boulders, cutting into the earthen banks as it meandered across the prairie.

Making camp not far from the waters edge, they scouted the area, carefully searching for tracks and soon found what they were looking for: a place where animals came to the river to drink. It was well marked with many tracks and trampled down grass. Taking refuge in a good hiding spot, the hunters sat and waited until near dusk. Their wait was rewarded with the appearance of two large mule deer. Two shots rang out! One deer fell, but the other leaped back into the trees and was off before another shot could be fired. The next day two antelope were added to the kill. After each animal was shot, they would skin it out. Then after cutting up the best parts of meat, wrap it into the skin making it easy to travel.

They stayed at camp one more night, keeping a large campfire going since the air was considerably colder than the evening before.

The following day they arrived back at the Stearns' homestead with plenty of meat for both of them to last awhile. Del and Gaylord set about cleaning and preparing the meat for storage. The most popular way of preserving meat was to cure it with salt brine. Cutting the meat up into ham size pieces (10 to 15 pounds), they put them into clean 45 gallon barrels half filled with the brine solution, (one cup of salt and a bit of vinegar per 2 gallons of water). The meat would have to soak in the covered barrels for at least five or six days before it was taken out, dried off and hung in the smoke house for another three days. Once the meat was smoked they would put it in flour sacks to keep the flies off, and then hang it up in the cold room. Smoked meat preserved this way would last a few months, and in the winter, even longer. By then it would be time for another hunting trip, anyway.

The next day, with all of the meat soaking in the salt brine, and with some of Bessie's home baked bread and cookies in his nap-sack, Del wandered on home. Along the way home he stopped at the Barnes family homestead. They were a young family who lived just south of him and their homestead was on the path leading into town. Del would usually check to see if they needed anything while he was going in for supplies and he would often stop with mail for the family on his way back home. Four little girls ran into the yard to greet him. The girls were normally shy and hesitant to speak to strangers, but they loved to see Del. Dropping off a sack of antelope meat to Mrs. Barnes, he declared that they just had too much to handle. The barrels wouldn't hold it all so he would be pleased if they would take it and cook some up for a good meal and preserve the rest for later. Even without a smoke house, if cured, it would last quite awhile.

As he arrived at his own place he was already thinking about when he could get back to the Red Deer River. It was to become a favorite place for Del to visit often.

# Chapter 13
## WINTER

el sat by his little stove where the coals burned brightly throwing out warm, comforting heat. On his crude tabletop, a lantern gave off needed light even though it was mid-morning. Outside his little humble abode the sky was a sunless, dark gray; an imminent snowstorm loomed overhead.

Winter had settled in quickly. It was cold, very cold. The wind blew incessantly. The coyotes could be heard yapping in the not far off distance. They made a lonesome eerie sound lulling him to sleep each night.

Working on the leather toggle of one of his snowshoes, he sat it down satisfied that it was repaired well. Throwing his heavy wool coat and hat on, snowshoes in hand, he stepped outside. Putting his feet into the snowshoes, he picked up his pack basket which hung from a nail just outside the door, and carefully worked his way over the deep settled snow to the creek side. Muskrats were caught in two different traps he had carefully laid out. Throwing the two rats in his pack basket he scouted the area for more. Back near the house he found he had snared a good size rabbit. The traps were not very successful today but the furs were soon added to the growing number of skins he already had stretched and drying. It was late when he finished working with the hides and he was hungry. Digging out potatoes and turnips from the root cellar he soon had a good rabbit stew brewing on top of the stove.

Outside, the storm had finally hit and raged around the sturdy little house. It was hours before the storm gave up. Bright little stars blinked here and there in the dark cloudless sky. Enjoying the stillness of the night air, Del moved heavy snow, shovel by shovel, making his pathway to the barn.

A low deep snarling growl caused him to look up from his task. A large gray intruder soundlessly stood watching him. Eye-to-eye the animal stared him down as large teeth appeared from under the curled lip. Fear leaped into Del's throat as his heart raced wildly. His rifle! Foolishly he had left the rifle inside the house. Never should he have ventured out at night without it. He raised his shovel and shouted. Again Del raised his shovel, yelling as he backed his way into the house. Finally, rifle in hand, he raced back outside, but the wolf was gone. The path was empty; silence surrounded him just as if nothing had ever been there.

Cautiously Del reached the barn. The animals were undisturbed. Lighting a lantern he talked to each of them as he worked, feeding them grain and cleaning the pens. He spoke soothingly to his little black and white pony as his hand combed her long black mane. Picking up the coarse bristled brush he worked on the animal, softly brushing her as he talked. She was the prettiest little pinto pony he had ever seen. He had found her in Oyen among a herd of young horses brought in for sale. His fingers traced the newly branded mark on her hindquarter. All of his cattle and horses had been branded with the combined DB using a backwards D.

Since 1878 it was required by law in the Northwest Territories (including what was to eventually become Alberta) to have livestock branded. Inflicting the pain of a burning hot iron on this little pony was difficult to bear. She had endured her fate well, just like a lady, he had thought to himself. Thus, he named his pretty pony, Lady. Owning such an animal gave him comfort.

The lonesome solitude of the cold winter days was working on him. The next day found Del packing his furs and heading to the trading post to turn them in. Finding neighbors and other farmers to pass the time with lifted his spirits and renewed his morale. The day slipped away fast and it was late when he headed toward home. Darkness had closed in as the bitter night air pierced through him.

The Stearns home came into view. It was always an open door for Del. He knew he was always welcome there. They were such kind hearted, friendly people that they could not help but take him in like one of their own family.

There were no lights in the windows; they had all gone to bed. Putting his horse in the barn, Del quietly tiptoed into the kitchen. Without disturbing anyone he climbed the ladder to the loft and found refuge for the night in the boys' bedroom. It was just like the warm comfort of home.

The aroma of coffee perking and bacon sizzling on the stove stirred Del's senses as he slowly awoke early the next morning. Quietly he tried to sneak down the ladder but a very startled Bessie watched him descend into the kitchen, her eyes as big as saucers.

"Why you devil you!" She exclaimed. "How on earth did you ever get up there? And when?"

"That coffee sure smells good!" Del said sheepishly, grinning from ear to ear. A lock of brown hair waved across his brow; soft hazel eyes twinkled in his boyish face. Bessie poured him a cup of coffee and told him to sit and tell her all about what he had been up to in town to cause him to be out so late.

"Well, you see" Del explained light heartedly. "I had to go do some celebrating last night. Yesterday was December 18 and it was my birthday."

Del had turned 26 years old.

# Chapter 14
## PA AND EMERY ARRIVE

Finally, the cottonwood trees started sprouting promising buds and the brush along the side of the creek became sprinkled with blossoms here and there. The cold nights turned to warmer days. Soft fresh rain soothed and nourished the dormant land. Bright sunlight created warm morning skies, deep blue with soft white clouds. The snow slowly disappeared and new life took hold. Spring had arrived in Alberta.

Prairie sod was soft from an early morning rain as Del slowly moved along, his horses pulling the wagon toward the railroad station in Alsask. Cool air brushed his face and filled his lungs. Overhead he could see birds soaring over the magnificent landscape. Soft greens of varied shades spread across the rolling terrain. Pa and brother Emery were arriving for their visit as promised, on the afternoon train. This spring morning, Del's spirits where high with anticipation as he traveled. He knew that once Pa made up his mind to visit he would make the trip without fail. Pa loved to travel and any excuse to see more of the country was all he needed to be on his way. Through many letters back and forth, it had been decided that Emery would try to build a homestead next to Del's. Emery was coming to stay.

Del had been to the land agent and made arrangements for the adjoining lot to be claimed in Emery's name. Now, between the two of them, they would have 320 acres of land. This piece of property had been abandoned some time ago. Someone had applied for the homestead but never developed it. After a time, it was turned back to the government and became available again. Knowing this property connected to his, Del wanted to file for it as quickly as possible for Emery. He came close to missing out on claiming this land, very close indeed. His thoughts moved back to that cold day in March when he arrived at the land agent's office in Oyen.

It was very early morning, well before it was time for the office to open.

He was early because he wanted to be the first one in the door to make his claim. He hadn't been waiting long when another fellow came along and also waited for the office to open. The two men sat down on the steps and began to talk. Soon the conversation got around to the property they were applying for. Looking at the land maps, the other man pointed at a lot number and said, "This is the one I want, it just became available and it's a good piece of property. Which one are you after?"

Del tried to act indifferent as he watched the man point to his lot number. Realizing that they were both after the same land, Del thought quickly.

"Well, I'm going to claim this lot over here," he said, pointing to a different lot number north of the one he really wanted.

"That's good." the guy said, "I was afraid you were after the same one I was."

To claim free land from the government was sometimes a battle. You had to be tough and you had to be shrewd to get what you wanted. This man was not his friend. He was a mere stranger; there was no need to be well mannered and gracious when it came to fighting for land. Del listened to the man talk while keeping a sharp ear toward the door, listening for the slightest chance that someone was there. He was on his feet and standing at the door as soon as the latch turned. He had been the first one to arrive; he should be the first one to see the agent. Without giving the stranger a backward glance he rushed to the office. He was the first to enter his claim for the land they both wanted.

Del could hardly contain his excitement as he watched his father and brother get off the train. Their five-day journey had finally brought them to their destination and left them weary and tired.

Emery was small in size for a young man of eighteen, quiet and very serious. His clothes were neat and worn with care and pride. Appearance meant a lot to him. An easy smile, quick to brighten his face, was often found.

Pa was a stern, sovereign man. His hair was thin, wavy white, matching a small mustache on his slender face. He was not easy to please, but was fair and quick with praise when it was due. He was used to traveling, but this was the longest journey he had ever ventured.

Loading the baggage into the wagon the three men soon headed for Del's homestead. Pa and Emery were amazed to find the path they followed simply meandered across the prairie. This was not what they would call a road. They followed the railroad track as far as it went. The line was extending west. It would soon be connected to Oyen and beyond. When the tracks ended they kept going west until Oyen came into site. From there they drove north, passing homestead after homestead.

Many of the homes they passed were simply built small structures or just sod huts. Cresting a small hill, Del pulled the horses to a stop. The slopping countryside gave view to his farm nestled along the creek. The property boasted a nice wood frame house, complete with windows, doors and a shingled roof. Cattle grazed inside a fenced-in yard beside a small barn.

"There it is!" Del announced with pride. "This is my Fair Acres."

Del's home was a sturdy, well built 16 x 24 wood frame structure. There was plenty of room upstairs where Pa and Emery were to sleep since there was only one bedroom downstairs. The barn was small but Del planned to add to it as soon as he could. The hand dug well was impressive and one of the best around.

Exploring both homesteads and trips into town filled the days of Pa's stay. They visited all the neighbors and enjoyed a large meal at Gaylord and Bessie Stearns home. Along the banks of the Red Deer River the three men enjoyed a feast of brown trout cooked over a campfire. They camped there, keeping the fire going, watching the night turn to day while talking and telling stories. Before long it was time for Pa to return home; Del and Emery had to begin working on their fields. Together they took Pa to the railroad station in Saskatchewan. He had a very long journey ahead of him. With mixed feelings of envy, jealousy and sadness Pa waved goodbye to his two sons as the train departed from the station. Part of him wanted to stay and share the adventures of this new land and homestead so different from his own; new territory to discover, explore and learn from. They were young and so many possibilities lay before them.

The wheels turned and the train sped east, rapidly taking him farther away. Pa settled back in his seat watching the prairie pass by the window. Slowly the envy vanished, replaced with pride. His boys would do well and make a place for themselves in this world. He soon recognized a deeper longing surfacing to take hold of his mind. In reality, a larger part of him yearned for the familiar surroundings of home and the family waiting for him there.

Baxter Family – Front Row – Delbert, Herbert, Ozmond, Pa (Laban)
Back Row -  Homer, Clint, Emery
Girl (sisters)  Luella, Mina

# Chapter 15
## EMERY

Emery rested his new fishing pole in the corner of the room. Picking up a box filled with odds and ends he began sorting items, tinkering at making up a few flies for the new pole. As he passed the time he watched Del whittle a piece of wood, turning it this way and that, until it grew into a nice piece. What the piece was for, he was not sure.

It was late evening, the chores were done, and evening light was growing dim with night moving in. Bored with the fly fishing project, Emery stood and faced the window. The scene before his eyes was a bleak, desolate, rolling countryside. Stepping outside he stood still with hands in his pocket. The night creatures were beginning to sing and hum as they filled the warm still air. Crickets and bugs came to life, spreading across the creek side. He listened carefully for the owl. Once in awhile the wise old bird would join in with a hoot-hoot. Tonight he was not there.

The cattle and horses wandered about the fenced in yard, content with their space. "That was it," Emery thought to himself. A meaning to his feelings seemed to surface. "They are content with their space." Del, too, seemed to be content and happy here. Maybe in time he would find that same sentiment. Right now, his own space seemed to be overshadowed with raw loneliness.

In the days that passed, Del and Emery had succeeded in working up more of Del's land and planting seed for grain. The first year Del was there, he plowed 15 acres and cropped 15 acres to seed. With Emery's help, he plowed 35 more acres and cropped the whole 50 acres. The days were hot and the work was hard. Guiding the walking plow through the fields behind the pair of oxen was slow drudgery. Under Del's instruction the plow had to be set deep. This prairie land was virgin soil; the first time to ever be tilled and the grass roots grew very deep. Sowing the seed was not much better, although the work was a tad easier. The shelter of a broad brimmed hat would shield his face from the intense rays of the sun as he walked the entire field broadcasting the seed. Dust seeped into the pores of his skin, filling his lungs and clogging his air passages. A heavy bag slung over one shoulder carried the seed that he flung by the handful; one to the right, one to the left of his path as he slowly went. A team of horses moved a bit faster than the oxen as they steadily pulled Del's homemade drag, covering this new seed into the earth.

Emery was restless. The work kept him busy but his young spirit needed more than work to be satisfied with this way of life.

On a mid-summer Saturday afternoon, Del and Emery drove the horses and wagon into Oyen to buy building supplies. The spring fieldwork was finished. It was time to begin working on Emery's claim. The two brothers could easily live together in Del's house, but some kind of building had to be constructed on the site for the homestead records.

The store clerk boxed up their supplies chatting with them as he did so. "You fellas should stick around town. There's going to be a boxing match at the livery stable tonight." Emery listened with renewed enthusiasm. This he had to see!

An odor of hay, horses and the sweat of human bodies filled the dim area of the barn. The double doors had been swung wide open to let in needed air and partial sunlight. A crowd of baying men, young and old, packed around the makeshift ring. Del and Emery made their way fervently through the mob, finally gaining a vantage point to watch the boxing match taking place. Cold hard cash had been laid down, betting on the outcome giving rise to frantic outbursts of frustration and anger.

Emery quietly looked on with total absorption. Flinching involuntarily, emotions clearly showed on his face as they watched. A young man was getting badly beaten, his bloodied face was the appearance of misery, but he wouldn't give up. His rival appeared to be older, bigger and was fighting dirty. As in most cases of "backyard" boxing, there were no rigid rules.... anything goes. A few low blows and that was the end of it. The young man, a mere boy really, lay face down on the dirt floor, coughing. Having reached beyond his limit, he did not try to get up. The local's cheered, sneered and shouted as a man named Johnson was declared the winner.

Watching his every move, Emery knew what he could have done; he could have beaten that guy.

"I want to do this," he told Del. "Just give me the chance!"

Before the night was through, Emery found himself in the ring. A pair of borrowed hand sewn leather gloves seemed well fitted as he tied the strings around his wrist. Emery stepped eagerly into the ring. His challenger was another young man about the same age and similar in size. As luck would have it, Emery had the advantage of experience. Boxing was something he use to fool around back home with his brothers and cousins for a pastime. Eyeing each other carefully, they danced around the ring throwing punches, calculating each others next move. By the end of the match, Emery emerged the winner with nothing more than a bloody nose and a bruised cheekbone.

As the two horses pulled the loaded-down wagon toward home through the darkness of night, Emery and Del talked and laughed playing the match over and over again. The twenty-mile trip seemed to pass in no time at all. Climbing into bed at last, a tired but exhilarated Emery found himself wide awake throughout the whole night, sleep eluding him entirely.

Del watched with amusement as Emery hopped around swinging one hand out and then the other, shadow boxing. Left punch, right punch, his feet swinging left to right as he went. As the summer wore on, the only thing that Emery took much interest in was boxing, although he and Del did enjoy a few hunting and fishing trips together. The regular Sunday get together with the Stearns and other neighbors playing horseshoes and baseball had been fun, too. Emery was a part of it all, but his heart just wasn't in it. When they were together working on the homestead, Emery remained quiet, distant; his mind on far off places more than in the present. Only the challenge of boxing kept his interest and he worked at it feverishly.

Summer days pushed on. Harvesting time came and went. Delivering the crop to the grain elevators provided a nice size voucher. The weeks and months of their labor had proved to be well satisfying. Evidence of autumn showed its face, replacing the warm succulent air surrounding the land with cold temperatures and blasts of frigid winds. Frost snuffed the life from all living foliage.

Arriving at a neighboring homestead, Emery was wholeheartedly ready for yet another fight at the home of the Johnson brothers. Del and Gaylord moved about pushing past a group of men in the crowd laying down bets. Hearing the jeers and guff, Emery was not favored to win. This was one fight Del did not want to see happen. A deep gut feeling told him that this was going to be bad. His anxiety was contagious as he and Gaylord waited with apprehension. The two contenders stepped into the temporary ring. Emery was no match for this sparring competitor. Billy Johnson was a natural bully, big and mean as the devil. Emery was fearless with confidence gained from his many successes over the summer as he nimbly moved, dancing around Billy. Suddenly they were knocking lumps out of each other. The gang of onlookers was going wild with each blow. Emery was taking the impact of almost every punch. Mercilessly, Billie worked him over hard and without hesitating, knocked Emery out cold in the second round.

Heat from the small stove furnished warm comfort as Emery rested his bruised body, sore and hurting from head to toe. The throbbing pain in his head had subsided and he craved a drink of cold water. Moving out of bed was difficult. Before he could reach the water jug Del was there getting it for him. Sitting down stiffly, clenching his hands around the cup, he slowly sipped the cool wet water. Accepting defeat was a jolt to his young ego, but Emery admitted he was very thankful to still be alive.

The newly built station in Oyen was busy as people milled about waiting for the morning train.

"One round-trip ticket for Massena, New York," Emery told the ticket-agent.

Del had a profound doubt that Emery would ever really want to return.

"Are you sure now, you want a round-trip ticket?"

"Oh yes, I will be back in the spring. I just need to see a little bit of home again for awhile." Emery replied, as he took Del's hand, shaking it slightly and giving his brother a quick hug. A slightly older, slightly wiser Emery stepped onto the waiting train. There were no signs of his wounds and he looked very handsome in his freshly starched shirt and Sunday-best suit jacket. A smile spread across his face as he looked Del in the eye.

"I'll be back to lick ole Johnson, wait and see!" With that, he stepped back into the passenger car and merely disappeared among the travelers.

# Chapter 16
## ROCKY MOUNTAIN HOUSE

Standing in the doorway, Del took one last look around. Everything was cleaned up and put away with nothing left out to attract rodents or varmints. He was a little worried about leaving his house empty for the whole winter. Outside the wind blew, whisking scattered snowflakes about. Mounting his horse, Del pulled up his coat collar protecting the back of his neck from the wind. Tugging his hat down tightly and picking up the reins, he began the trek of herding his little band of animals south to Gaylord Stearns' place. The scruffy little packhorse followed faithfully along, but Del grabbed the reins of his pinto pony to keep her in line. The oxen and cattle moved about sullenly, reluctant to leave the confines of their pens.

Winters on the homestead were long, harsh and lonesome. Many of the young men from the area spent the cold months working in far off logging camps high up in remote areas of the mountains. Work that would keep him busy, pass the time away. Besides the money was good, a high wage was paid for driving oxen in a lumber camp.

When Del had read the ad for workers needed in the camps, his mind raced. Many winter months had been spent in a lumber camp in the far off Adirondacks ever since he was old enough to work. There, Pa, his older brothers Ozzie and Herb, and many of his uncles and cousins all worked together. Usually the logs where driven out of the woods to a railroad station by a large horse drawn flat bed sleigh. At times they were able to float logs down the Raquette River to their destination, a mill located miles down the mountainous river channel. Del knew this kind of work. A winter in a logging camp would be a welcoming change from the prairie life.

Rocky Mountain House; he had no idea where this was but with a little bit of inquiring he soon found someone who did.

Inside the general store a group of aged men sat around the pot-bellied stove, slipping away lingering hours. Soaking up warmth and comfort, they seemed to have nothing more to do with their time than smoke corncob pipes and watch the people come and go. An ancient miner sitting among them had been there and he knew this place well. His wrinkled face broke into a grin, dark eyes lit up as he took the opportunity to provide his knowledge of this far off place. With an aura of importance, he began to recall buried memories of times past.

"It's far off, two hundred fifty miles west of here. Out-of-the-way place to be found on the North Saskatchewan River. The old trails were rough and long. Luckily, now the train runs right through that area, going to Rocky Mountain House and clear beyond."

"It's an odd name for a town." Del said as he sat down in a chair next to the old miner. His attention had been captured; he listened closely to what the old man had to say.

"Ya, it's an odd name fer a town but there's a story to that," he was eager to explain. "Twas an old fort startin back in the 1700's, first made into a tradin post for the Hudson Bay Company. A trapper fixed it a name in 1802 "Rocky," for the rocky formation of the riverbed there and "Mountain," for the beautiful view of the mountains from the point. "House" was the usual title of a fur tradin-post. It's a long name, but a good one; a name to be remembered.

It's a place of legends. They say ancient Indians gifted it with magic, a spell placed back beyond the time of white man. You take heed of my words, if you travel to this place called Rocky Mountain House, there's some kind of witchery there."

"The folks there are plenty friendly to strangers," he continued. "Lots of Indian people. Their village is not far off from the town. It was once known as Blackfoot country, but many years ago there was a great war with the Cree. The Blackfoot in that area were fully wiped out."

The old codger's folded hands lay across a round belly as he tilted back in his wooden chair. It creaked under the weight as he talked on, telling his story.

"In 1875 the tradin post closed down. No white man lived there again till about 1904 or so when set'lers started moving in. They came from Ontario and other points east and from the old countries across the ocean: Italy, Germany, Austria, Sweden, to name a few. A good settlement was being built up at Red Deer at that time, the end of the line for the C.P.R. But some of these early set'lers weren't content to stay there so they packed up and pushed on deeper into the mountainous territory – all the way to Rocky Mountain House - sixty miles away from the railroad. Bout 1910 or 12 the CPR built on through the town and ended at Nordegg. That's fifty miles west of Rocky

Mountain House. Plenty of wood trade, logging for railroad ties, posts, fencing and building lumber. And there's the coal mining, too."

"And another warning to ya," he went on as an afterthought, "Don't ever travel the train to Rocky Mountain House on a Wednesday!" The old man chuckled merrily with this thought amusing him but he would not give any reason; "you'll see" is all he would say as his belly shook with laughter.

The old miner's story ran through Del's mind as the railroad car gently swayed back and forth. His thoughts blended with the steady groan of clicking wheels moving along the tracks. As the engine puffed and chugged leaving the plains behind, the train climbed steadily to where the prairie met the mountains. Small herds of antelope could often be seen grazing on the grasses off in the distance and even a small herd of buffalo passed by the window very close to the tracks. Sighting a herd of buffalo was rare in those days. Del watched as the large hairy animals moved together. One lone bull displayed a long beard from his massive head, watching over his small band of four or five females. At one time great herds of these grand beasts covered the prairies. Now they were reduced to these unusually tiny packs, clinging to existence. Across the horizon he watched the mountain peaks rising above the plains through the dense billowing smoke of the grand steam engine.

This is where Rocky Mountain House was to be found, in the foothills of the great Rockies of Alberta. A small town nestled among rocks and trees where the Clearwater River joins the Great North Saskatchewan.

As Del stepped off the train onto the platform of the depot, he wondered what all the mystery of this place could be. The station was rather new, with

Rocky Mountain House boldly printed across the front. The rest of the town looked drab and lifeless. Stark small wood frame buildings strung along a dirt street. They seemed not much more than shacks to him. A long narrow boardwalk lined the fronts of the main street buildings. Homes dotted about around the town. Maybe it was the time of year, maybe it was the mountains, but an air of cold desolation hovered about. He could feel no Indian magic, no witchery here, only a cold blast of wind pushing at his back.

A small hotel seemed to be the focal point of town. A rush of friendly faces greeted him warmly. He found a room, a bath, and a good hot meal of baked moose meat with dumplings and berry pie. The energy and friendliness floating about became contagious. After the meal had been served, the cook walked about talking to customers, telling stories and laughing at his own jokes. Obviously of a mixed Indian descent, his black hair fell down his back in a long ponytail; beads adorned a large solid neck. Del found himself grinning and laughing out loud easily. Others would join in competing for the best tales to be told. Tales of the old Hogopogo of the North Saskatchewan were shared. Many had heard of this fierce and terrifying river monster, and a few claimed to have seen it. Chief Walking Eagle was the first to discover the monster's existence and there was not a soul around who would dispute his word.

When the evening had passed, Del had a warm contented feeling within. His single room with the small bed and meager furnishings was warm, cozy and comfortable. Sleep came easily. He had found the town's spell; the Indian magic was here after all. Within the drab walls with the look of bleak existence, the spell consumed the weary traveler who welcomed it with an open embrace.

Main Street, Rocky Mountain House

# Chapter 17
## LIFE IN A LOGGING CAMP

Awell-worn trail led through the tall timbers a few miles back to a logging camp, a large log building with a bunkroom and a dinning hall. Del found work there driving a team of oxen pulling loads of long, fresh cut logs. The lumberjacks were a mixture of every sort. Many were young men like him, farmers here for the winter months among hard, burly woodsmen of the north. Some were of native Indian descent; others were foreigners speaking with thick accents.

Del roused sleepily to loud shouts of "Daylight in the swamp!" as the camp boss bellowed from the doorway of the bunkroom. In the darkness he fumbled for his clothes while others muttered mostly unintelligible moans and sighs. Someone lit a lantern as they all moved about waking up, it was 5:00 am.

Hot thick pancakes covered with dark rich syrup, fat sausage patties and strong coffee were served in the big hall as the men gathered about the long tables. With breakfast over, they collected their tools and equipment and headed out to the big woods, ready to begin their various jobs.

Before the first of the workers had begun to appear outside, Del had made his way to the barn. Having fed and watered all of the animals, he led a pair of oxen outside to be hitched up to the large sleigh used to carry the heavy loads of logs out of the woods.

The morning passed and at noon the cook arrived at the worksite driving a short, horse drawn sled with lunch for all. Sitting around on stumps, rocks and logs they gobbled down their lunch and slurped hot coffee. The break was short and soon they were back to their jobs. Climbing on board the sleigh loaded down with long timber, Del reined the oxen onto the rough logging road and headed down the mountainside toward the mill to be unloaded. At this mill, the logs would be made into railroad ties and shipped out across the country. Tall timbers of every sort, reaching high into a deep gray sky, surrounded the trail. The lack of clouds and sunshine predicted more snowfall. A thick deep snow already covered the ground where large hills and rocks made up the countryside. The hard work filled the days and there was no time to be lonely.

Darkness moved in early on these cold winter days. But the workday did not end with the onset of darkness. Back at the camp house, Del and the other men pulled off damp wool clothes and wet boots, changing into warm, dry clothes. All around the heating stove in the bunkhouse they hung pants, shirts and boots to dry.

After changing his clothes Del left the clamor and commotion behind and headed to the barn. Enjoying the quiet, solitude of the animals' shed he caringly tended to the oxen and horses, carrying water and feeding them for the night. He had been more than happy to take over the responsibility of caring for the animals. While he did his chores, others had their own jobs. A few of the men put away equipment, while others sharpened axes on the grindstone. The blacksmith started repair work and the saw filer sharpened saws for the next day.

By 7:00 p.m. all was done and supper was ready. At last their workday had come to an end. After the big hot meal the men were ready to relax the way they new best. The large potbelly stove in the center of the hall was surrounded with chairs where men sat around and talked about the day and troubles of the world. A lone harmonica filled the room with a bright melody and soon a fiddle joined in. The music brightened their spirits and some of the men began to stomp and dance around the room. Del could do a little step dance himself. Jigging about with a skip and a jump he would click his heels. He was so sprightly and quick he made it look like he could click his heels twice before his feet landed back on the floor. You had to watch closely to see that he was actually tapping first his toes, then his heels. With much encouragement he put on a little show for the crew while they clapped their hands and hooted loudly.

Saturday nights most of the men would pile into big bobsleds and head for town. The soft lights glowing in the windows of homes and shops of the town were inviting. The men were ready for some distraction and entertainment. The hotel would soon be bursting with noise and spewing music from the old upright piano. After awhile, the music and merriment would die down and an old Indian would walk around the room and begin to tell his stories. A hush would fall about as they listened with fascination to this storyteller. He would charm his listeners with old and new legends that were comparable to the great Paul Bunyan and his big blue ox. Every week they would learn about different people in the past. David Thompson was a great celebrity; an early explorer who wintered at the fort in Rocky Mountain House while working his way west to discover a path to the Pacific Ocean. Only the chimneys of the old fort were standing now close to Pangman's Pine. Peter Pangman was the first white man to reach the site. He had inscribed his name on a tree near the river edge, thus giving the name to this great pine tree still standing.

Near these forsaken chimneys it was told that treasures where buried by traders living at the fort. Early in the 1820's, the Blackfoot dominated the area. They were a quarrelsome tribe, not getting along with other tribes or with the white man. For some small grievance against the traders, they held a council of war and made plans to attack the fort in the night and scalp the white man. Fortunately, a young brave who had been befriended by the traders slipped away and warned them. When the war party arrived, the fort was empty. The traders had fled. Before going they had buried as much of their supplies and furnishings as they could, including a keg of rum. To that day, the very aged rum had not been found.

[2]A most enduring story was about a Chief Jim O'Chase of the Chippewas. When the chief was a lad of seven, his band was camped in the hills along the Red Deer River. A scout discovered hostile Indians were watching the camp. In the darkness of the night, the Chippewas moved away to safety. It was not until late the next morning that they discovered the young boy was missing. He had become separated from the others in the darkness. The boy took shelter under some brushes and when he awoke, a big bull buffalo was nosing him about. He followed the buffalo herd all summer, snuggling up to their shaggy bodies for warmth during the night. Late the next fall his family, still searching for the missing boy, heard him whimpering in a dense scrubby gully. There they found Jim O'Chase alive and well. He told his family that his buffalo friends had deserted him that morning, when human help was within reach.

The loggers would end up spending the entire night having a good time at the hotel mingling and enjoying the town's people. Sunday mornings they would slowly mosey back to camp, settle in and get ready for work again on Monday.

The days and weeks turned into months with a blur. Winter passed and spring arrived early. Del knew he should soon head back to his little farm on the prairie. He couldn't delay much longer. His time here with the logging crew had come to an end. But, before he could go home, he had one more job to complete.

There were several oxen at the camp. The pair that Del drove each day

---

2    Johnny Chinook Tall Tales and True From The Canadian West, By Robert Gard, Published 1945 by Longmans, Green & Company. Stories reprinted with the permission of the Estate of Robert E Gard.

were the oldest and had lived well beyond their prime. The camp boss was concerned that they would not make it through another year pulling the large heavy loads. The camp cook was from the area and his father had offered to buy the oxen. He could use them on his farm where the work would not be as strenuous as pulling the heavy loads of logs day after day. They could continue to work and be useful for many more years.

Del had already put off going back and now this little project would way lay him even more. He would miss the deadline to pick up the government seed for his crops. But Del had cared for these animals all winter and the boss wanted him to take the responsibility of delivering them to their final home. A few extra dollars helped persuade him and Cookie even lent him his own horse on which to travel. Before Del could do this, he first had to make a trip back into town to find someone who would know what he could do about picking up his crop seed.

The friendly people of the little community were eager to help him. A bank clerk directed him to the local justice of the peace. This was the closest thing to a lawyer that lived in this town. He made out a paper for Del to sign giving Gaylord Stearns his power of attorney to pick up his share of the seed. It was as simple as that; Del would mail it to Gaylord and Gaylord would file the papers at the land office and have his seed ready for him when he got home.

The route through the tall thick forest was narrow; few had traveled this way since winter had settled in. Melting snow and fresh tepid air with a soft scent of newness covered the earth. Debris from fallen rotted branches and trees cluttered areas of the path. Budding wildlife chattered and chanted back and forth. Birds, brave enough to survive throughout the winter months in this deep mountain woodland, flitted from tree to tree chirping and whistling. A bright sun softened the sharpness of the cool air as Del carefully maneuvered his horse around the rubble of twigs and decayed logs. The oxen, moving in their heavy gate, slowly followed behind. The trail followed the river as closely as possible around the rocks and through the gullies along the mountain. Coming into a clearing, the trail ended at the waters' edge and it was here they must cross the river to reach their destination.

A large wooden barge used as a ferry, had been drawn up onto the shore to keep it high and dry for the winter. Connected to a pole was a heavy steel cable, which ran across the water to the other shore. Although the water was running freely and clear of ice, no one was around nor was the ferry open.

Reaching the river's edge, Del looked over the ferry crossing contemplating what to do. He could put the barge into the water, using the cable to pull them across by himself. But, unfortunately, the docks on the other side had also been taken out and moved up on land. The animals would have to swim part way to shore. This was the only way to cross this river and he knew that these oxen were not going to go willingly. He had to make a plan that would get these oxen to do what he needed. An idea came to mind, but it would take a little time. Well, he had time. There was no big rush to cross today.

Knowing the oxen would want to drink as soon as they saw the water, Del tied them to a tree. They could see the water but not get close enough to drink it. He made camp where a small cove lined with brush gave him shelter from the wind. Searching the woods he found a couple of young trees that were just small enough around for what he needed. Chopping them down with his small hatchet and trimming the branches, he ended up with two good long poles. He left the poles next to the big barge and then went about fixing a campfire and cooking his supper. He fed the animals some grain but was careful not to give the oxen any water. Before nightfall moved in, he found some long sturdy sticks and using a canvas tarp, made a rugged lean-to close to the fire. After gathering wood he sat on a spread out blanket, soaked up the warmth of the fire and listened to the noises of the forest.

Watching the river, he thought about the many tales he had heard about the great North Saskatchewan. There was gold in this river. And not far away in these hills was a mysterious gold mine. A site of betrayal, murder and madness, the mine was lost almost as soon as it was discovered. The native Indians said it carries a curse. Over the years many men, white, red and black, have died searching in vain for it.

[3]The story goes: two young Indian lads had followed two prospectors to a spot deep within a canyon where the men discovered the gold rich vein. They watched as one murdered the other and then fled in the aftermath of horror over what he had done. Arriving back at his fort, the remaining prospector confided to a missionary priest. The priest convinced him to lead others to where he had found the gold. But, every time they began to get close to the gold, the tortured prospector would go crazy in the head. He eventually became a complete raving lunatic. The young Indians who had watched the murder went back to their village and told their chief what they had seen. The great wise chief told them to never tell another soul of the whereabouts of this gold. As time went on and the lads became leaders of their men, they held their secret, carrying it to their grave.

Placing more wood on his campfire, Del rolled up the end of his blanket for a pillow. Using his other warm wool blanket as a cover, he curled up and was soon lulled to sleep by the soft sound of the river flowing through the darkness.

Early in the morning, Del used his long poles to pry up the heavy barge

3   Johnny Chinook Tall Tales and True from the Canadian West, by Robert Gard, Published 1945 by Longmans, Green & Company. Stories reprinted with the permission of the Estate of Robert E. Gard.

and move it into the water, tying it securely to the existing pier. After working the heavy ramp carefully into place, the ferry was ready to go. He led each of the oxen, slowly walking them onto the barge, not letting them get close enough to drink out of the river. With the oxen and his pony securely on board, he untied the barge and pushed off. Slowly but steadily, the ferry floated across the waters as Del pulled them along with the cable.

Reaching the other side, Del maneuvered the ferry as close to shore as possible, jumped out and tied it off. The horse, with a little persuasion, also jumped into the river and swam ashore. The stubborn oxen would not move, so he led them close to the edge of the barge. As he was hoping, they were so thirsty the two oxen dropped to their knees, stretched their necks to the water and began to drink. As soon as they did this, Del gave a big yell and snapped them with the bullwhip. The big clumsy animals jumped into the water and soon made their way to shore.

With the oxen delivered to the farmer, Del made his way back to the logging camp and returned the horse to Cookie. Packing up his things, he said his good-byes and headed into town to catch the train, which would eventually carry him back to Oyen and his prairie home.

This particular day happened to be a Wednesday. The street was filled with farmers and squealing, wailing, stinking pigs. Suddenly Del remembered the warning from the old miner back at Oyen's store, to never ride the train to Rocky Mountain House on a Wednesday. Now he knew why. Wednesday was pig day! Pigs were being driven right down the main street from all directions.

Pigs to be bought and sold; pig raising was a thriving business for the area. Wagons lined the streets with pig farmers loading or unloading. The train was filled with mixed freight, passengers and pigs, stopping at every siding to pick up more pigs.

Del laughed out loud as he hurried toward the depot. The conductor shouted, "All aboard!" and the whistle blew long and hard as the steam engine chugged, pulling out from the station. From his seat among the farmers, Del watched the little town of Rocky Mountain House fade into the deep forest and hills. He would miss the friendliness and special atmosphere that had welcomed him. He would never forget this place of magically enchanting stories and legends.

# Chapter 18
## CLINT

It was well into spring by the time Del arrived back at his little homestead. Gaylord met him at the railroad station and brought him home where Bessie was waiting for them. Bessie made a big fuss over him and outdid herself cooking up a big meal for his homecoming. As they enjoyed the food, they talked and laughed as Del shared his many experiences. Later while relaxing in the comfort of the Stearns' parlor, Del sorted out the pile of mail that Gaylord had collected. Quickly he tore open a letter from home, expecting to find some news of Emery coming back. Gaylord was watching as he folded the letter, placing it back in the envelope. Glancing up, Del looked at Gaylord and let out a big sigh.

"Emery is not coming back. I'm not surprised at that. But," he said with a change of heartiness in his voice, "Clint's going to use his return ticket and come out for a visit. Clint's my younger brother." Del explained as he chuckled softly. "He's a great kid, you will like him. I can't believe he's going to make the trip all the way out here by himself!"

Del didn't dwell on his disappointment of Emery not returning, throwing away his homestead and a chance at a life in the west. Del had high hopes and big plans, thinking the two brothers would work together and make a good size farm with their combined property. It was a great idea, but it just wasn't going to work out the way Del had hoped. Plenty of work was waiting for him and he wanted to get the place ready before it was time for Clint to arrive. It would be fun to have Clint here, and that was something to look forward to.

From the very moment that Clint arrived, he was in love with the prairie. At seventeen he was tall, lanky and hadn't quite grown into his large frame. He was already taller than Del and still had years of growing. His happy-go-lucky, carefree nature and cheerfulness was infectious. He was more than excited to be there. Meeting the people, learning about the land, everything so new and different was completely awesome. He cheerfully worked along with Del, was eager to help and always ready to do more.

Clint could never catch a fish with a hook and line. Wading into the shallow waters of the brook he had great luck at spearing. He would take his catch back for Del to clean and cook. Clint never liked the taste of fish much, but Del sure loved them.

Everyday at the first break of dawn, Clint would be out with the shotgun moving carefully along the brook waiting and watching for ducks or geese. Usually he would see nothing but frogs, birds and lots of mosquitoes. It was about two weeks into his visit when his luck turned. He was out early as usual, as the sunlight began to streak across a wide sky, turning dim gray to bright blue. He didn't have long to wait. A flock of ducks fluttered their wings and splashed gracefully into the water not far upstream. Del smiled as he watched Clint walk toward the barn with two ducks dangling from his hands. He decided it was time to take that big camping trip and show Clint some of the country. The spring plowing and planting was finished. Now would be the best time to go.

They packed up the camping gear, and prepared some food. Clint watched as Del brought out his little bag of flour and mixed baking power and salt with it.

"What ya doing that for?"

"Biscuits." Del answered. "When we get hungry and are ready to eat all I have to do is stir them up with a little bit of water"

The top of the flour bag would serve as his mixing bowl. When they were ready to fix up some food he would make a little pocket in the top of the flour, pour in just a little bit of water, and stir gently until it was thick enough to make his biscuits.

With the packhorse loaded down with camping gear and rifles the two mounted their horses and headed north.

They hadn't gone far when they came to the Barnes family home. They stopped and went inside just as the family was sitting down to breakfast. Around the square table quietly sat four little blonde girls. Each had their hair pulled back in long braids and their big blue eyes stared at them with curiosity. Mrs. Barnes graciously invited them to eat.

No, they wouldn't stay, but just wanted to let Mr. Barnes know that they were leaving. He was going to watch over the place and the animals while they were gone.

They rode out into the countryside with the sun at their backs. Del had been through this country before on hunting trips, but it was all a new experience to Clint. They had been riding a few hours when off in the distance a group of trees and shrubs came into view. The grass grew longer and thicker and as they neared, they could see it was a lake.

Looking at Del a bright grin spread across Clint's face. "I'll race ya there!" he yelled as he slapped his horse and was off before all the words were out of his mouth. The horse stretched easily as his muscles worked hard with every stride. Clint leaned close to his neck whispering "go boy, go!" giving him full rein. Horse and rider raced through the grassland with graceful speed. Clint loved nothing more than a good horse and he could outride the best of cowboys. Del let his horse go, hoofs pounding into the dry sod, rising to the challenge but Clint's lead was too big.

Reaching the shore, Clint pulled up the reins and stopped short. Swinging down off the saddle he patted the horse's neck and held his bridle tight as the horse tried to reach for a drink of the water. Clint looked around in awe. The rocks and ground the length of the shoreline were covered with a pure white gritty crust. There were some animal bones strewn about the area.

"What is it?" He asked as Del came up behind him.

"It's salt," Del replied, getting down off his horse. " A salt lake. We can't let the horses drink here, its not good for them. Clint had never seen anything like it, nor heard about any such thing as a lake filled with salt.

Warily they led the horses away from the unsafe waters. They walked for a ways giving the horses a break, leading them back toward the trail. As they walked together side by side, Del explained what he knew.

"It's a small lake and has no outlet, no river drains from it. It has a salty basin and over time the salts have absorbed into the water enough to make it a salt lake. It would be the same as drinking water from the ocean."

They traveled on enjoying the ride and the company of each other. Later in the day they came upon a herd of half a dozen pronghorn antelope feeding off sagebrush. Dropping into a coulee, the men waited and stalked the herd. Antelope are quick and can run fast. Before the antelope got a look at them, Clint took one down with skill and accuracy. Working together they dressed it out and cut up some meat for their supper.

They soon came to a small stream. The horses were allowed to drink their fill and the men set up camp for the night. While Del took care of the horses, Clint found a little wood near the stream and made a fire. They unpacked the pan and kettle and set about to cook the antelope. Del showed Clint how he stirred up the biscuits and put them in the pan to cook. While they were cooking they put water on to boil for coffee. Clint helped himself to a fresh biscuit while the antelope cooked, praising Del for his creative cooking ability.

For several days the two brothers traveled on this way. It was late one afternoon when they came upon a large ranch and trading post. It was here they met up with a group of fur traders. They all sat around and talked, swapping stories and tall tales. Most of these trappers had been out in the wild country all winter and were hungry for news of other places. A few of the men had been living and trapping very far up north in the high mountains of the Northwest Territory. They talked about a most beautiful country with all kinds of wild life. Peace River Country they called it.

As Del listened to the men talk of life in the mountains, a seed was planted. A hunger to see such a place began to grow deep inside. Little did he know these stories would be the beginning of a new restlessness for him, a beginning of the end of his contentment with prairie life.

Del and Clint spent the night at the ranch, paying 25 cents for a room and boarding their horses.　　　 Leaving early the next morning they started working toward home but took a different route to see more of the country. Along the way they came to a place that looked abandoned. So many times a homestead family would simply pack up and leave behind all they had worked for and dreamed of. The harsh reality and loneliness was just too much for them.

A tiny shack stood by itself against the bleak surroundings. Behind it was a shed for the horses. A tall slope of land sheltered the house from the sun. A small patch of ground on the side of the house looked soft, as though it might have been a one-time garden.

A cook stove was the only thing left inside the shack. It must have been too big and heavy for the people to take with them. Checking the stove out Del decided it was in working condition with enough coal left to use. He started to prepare some food for supper when he thought about the patch of old garden. Using his ax, he dug around in what looked like potato hills. Chopping into the ground, sure enough, he found potatoes still there. A little more digging about gave him fresh onions and a few turnips. What a feast they would have now! Cleaning up the vegetables he put them in the kettle with cured bacon for flavor and cooked a very nice stew, along with the biscuits, too, of course. What a treat after so many days camping out.

Plenty of work was waiting for Del and Clint when they returned to the homestead. The long days became hot and dry with little rain.

It was mid-morning on a day that threatened to be hotter than usual. Clint was on the south side of the property building new fences. Gray clouds drifting in looked promising for needed rain. As he worked, concentrating on digging postholes with a large iron bar, Clint paid no attention to the sky. Pulling his shirttail out from under his bibbed overhauls he wiped the sweat off his forehead. A sharp clap of thunder surprised him. His eyes searched the sky overhead as a gust of wind swept in a light rain. He had worked his way a distance from the farm as the fence he was building bordered the Barnes' property line. Picking up the large iron bar, he slung it over his shoulder and began to walk toward home.

A streak of lightening flashed before his eyes and suddenly the ground came right up and hit him. The drizzling rain fell as he lay on the ground for just an instant. Dazed and confused he jumped to his feet and began running. Clint made a beeline for the Barnes' house. Still in shock he burst through the door, ran right past the four little girls, into the kitchen and there he hid behind the cookstove.

Clint sat on the floor, his big frame curled up like a small child. He soon began to regain his senses but still was not sure what had happened to him. A startled Mrs. Barnes watched Clint with alarm. Then, hearing her husband yelling from outside, she grabbed a broom from the corner and ran out of the house. Slowly Clint stood and walked to the door. The prairie grass was on fire. Small streaks of flames were spreading fast. Mr. Barnes was already fighting the fire as his wife joined in beating at the flames with her broom. Clint grabbed a shovel out of the shed and started pounding on the racing sparks along beside his neighbors. They managed to put the flames out before it had grown to a raging uncontrollable prairie fire, saving the house and barns and possibly even their lives. Like most prairie homes, Mr. Barnes had plowed a large furrow around his house and animal shed. This left nothing for the fire to burn on the furrow but dry dirt. This was the best protection a farmer had from the dreaded prairie fires.

Clint was lucky to have survived his ordeal without suffering from any ill effects at all. For many years to come he would tell his story about being struck by lightening out on the prairie lands of Alberta, Canada.

It was a short time later they received a letter from Pa. Inside the letter was a train ticket. The summer days had moved on and the hay fields were tall, thick and ready for mowing back in New York. Pa needed help and it was time for Clint to go home.

# Chapter 19

## THE ACCIDENT

After Clint left, the little house seemed empty; suffocating silence hung heavy in the air. Del missed his brother bustling about and talking constantly. He had never noticed the solitude as much as he did now. The days and nights became long and Del filled the hours working steadily on his farm. Before long the thrashers arrived, harvested his fields and moved on to the next homestead. The pigs had grown big and fat; they were ready to be taken to market.

With the summer's end, Del decided on a building project to add on to his barn before winter. He had been marking off the dimensions for this project so that he would have an idea of how much lumber he would need. A trip into town had been planned for the next day along with his neighbors, Ben Alden, Stan Barnes and Gaylord. They were all going to help Del take the pigs into town for the livestock sale and also pick up a winter supply of coal while they were there. Del figured he could bring back a good amount of building lumber at the same time. The building project would give him something to work on and stay busy. Finishing up his measurements he went about feeding the cattle and horses. The pigs swaddled about in their pens, grunting and snorting, groveling for food as they always did as soon as they saw him.

With the chores done he leaned on the fence rail chewing on the end of a long piece of hay while looking out over his fields. The long warm days had dragged on with little rain. The crops hadn't done well and the check for the grain had been slim. It looked like he would have to depend on another winter at Rocky Mountain House to make some money. He grinned at the thought; he had been planning on it anyway. It seemed he enjoyed the life of a logger more than a farmer. A prairie farmer's life was difficult but the mountains were something else. Now there was a life.

Early the following morning Del was just hitching up the oxen to the wagon when Ben and Stan drove up; each with a team of oxen pulling their wagons. It took awhile for the three men to get all of the pigs herded into the wagons but before too long they were ready to go. Reaching Gaylord's place they pulled up into his yard. Gaylord was ready and waiting for his neighbors: Bessie had just finished packing a basket of food for him with enough for the others too. Although they no longer had to make the fifty-mile journey to Alsask to meet the coal train, it would still be a long trip. It took most of the day just to ride into Oyen with the slow moving oxen. They arrived in time to unload the pigs at the livestock sale pens. Once the pigs were unloaded, the men moved their wagons into an empty field and proceeded to clean them out. They used many buckets of water washing them down after shoveling and scraping to get rid of the stench and foul droppings left behind by the pigs. Del did his business with the cattle dealer while the others headed the clean wagons over to the coal train. Gaylord tied Del's team to the back of his wagon so that he could lead them together and join the line to wait their turn. The four men camped by their wagons. It was well into the following day before they were loaded up and able to start for home.

The wagon was already heavy with coal but Del was determined to take some lumber home too. Placing the boards very carefully along the length of the wagon the pile seemed high but steady. They all helped him stack the pile on, but his neighbor's were skeptical that he would make it all the way back without losing some off the wagon. " Might as well make the most out of the trip." Del said as he climbed up, sat on top of the boards and started the oxen moving. For most of the way the trip went smoothly, the day had been long and tiring. They rode along in silence. Del was working out in his mind how he would build the addition to his barn.

A bump in the trail, and the wagon jostled just enough. The top of the lumber began to shift; one board began to slide and then another. The whole load of lumber was sliding to the ground. As the boards moved beneath him Del helplessly fell along with them. As he lay on the ground more boards landed on top of him. The oxen came to a stop, the wagon with its load of coal stood still; Del lay motionless among the boards that were strewn about. Gaylord, Ben and Stan all jumped off their wagons and rushed to help. Pulling the lumber off from Del they could see his face was already bruised and swollen. He started to move and grimaced in pain. Sharp pains shot threw his body from head to toe.

The next conscious moment Del had was much later. He felt comfortable, warm and a sense of being cared for, as he drowsily lay in bed and tried to open his eyes. Voices from the other room were fuzzy and he couldn't make out what they were saying. For a few fleeting seconds, just before he gained full consciousness, he thought he was home. Home, back on his parent's farm with Pa and Mother talking in hushed voices. The smell of the cookstove and the warm comfort of the blankets soothed his mind; he wanted nothing more than to float back into sleep again. Soon he was awake enough to realize that he was not in his parents' home, nor was he in his own bed, in his own house. Sharp pain bit into him as he tried to move his body and a dull ache surrounded his head. It was Gaylord and Bessie's voices drifting from the kitchen of their home.

He found that if he lay very still there was not much pain other than the constant ache in his head. Closing his eyes he remembered the lumber shifting, sliding to the ground as he helplessly fell off the wagon with it. That was all he could remember. He felt angry. Angry with himself for it was a foolish thing to do. A lazy man's load his pa would say. He was so sure he could take all that lumber home, piled on top of the load of coal. It doesn't pay to be so smart!

Del must have slept more, when he opened his eyes again Bessie was there checking on him.

"Hi there beautiful, what ya doing in a man's bedroom?" He tried to tease, but as he grinned it made his head hurt more.

"Ohhh" he moaned involuntarily.

"You have a concussion Del" Bessie sat in the chair beside the bed, picked up a soft damp cloth and wiped his face softly without touching the bruises. "Your head will ache for awhile but it will go away soon." Her voice was soft, filled with caring and pity. When they first carried Del into the house, Bessie was afraid his injuries were much more serious. She could not have cared for him more than if he were her own brother. She and Gaylord were greatly relieved when the doctor announced that Del's wounds were minor and he would survive.

Gaylord, hearing them talking, entered the room and stood looking down at Del, shaking his head back and forth. "You sure did a good job of banging yourself up. Poor Ben thought you was dead."

"I know I'm alive." Del said slowly "I feel every bone in my body."

"Got the doc out here to check you out." Said Gaylord. "He says you'll be alright but you have some cracked ribs and a broken collar bone and its going to take a while to heal. You're mighty lucky that's all you broke."

"Collar bone? Now what is a dang collarbone and where is it? Bessie pointed to the bone at the base of his neck and as he moved just slightly Del could feel the pain and knew exactly where the broken bone was.

"There's no way you can go home all by yourself, so you're going to stay right here with us until your healed. Gaylord and the boys got a bed set up for you in the front room. We'll get you moved out there as soon as you're able to move around a little. Right now I'm going to fetch some of my soup and get you some supper." Bessie's skirts rustled as she scurried out of the bedroom and into the kitchen. There was no arguing with Bessie. Del knew that he might as well save his breath. It hurt to talk much right now anyway and the smell of that soup, simmering on the stove, was making him hungry.

# Chapter 20
## Winter with the Stearns

**W**ounds heal and bones mend in good time. Del spent many months at the Stearns' home and it was deep into winter before he began to feel like his old self again. The doctor had fixed him up with a sling for his left arm and had ordered twelve weeks of rest for the broken collarbone. Bessie's good care and the family's company kept up his spirits. Bessie was always bright and cheerful. Del was sure there was not a thing, ever, in the world that she couldn't find something to be happy about.

For the first few weeks Del brooded and was down in the dumps. He didn't want to be a bother to anyone and wasn't happy being waited on. He had really been looking forward to going back to Rocky Mountain House. He was missing a whole winter's work in the logging camp, and for what? All for one foolish mistake. Now, instead of working outside in the fresh cold air making good money, he was laid up feeling lazy and sorry for himself. There was nobody to blame but himself. He couldn't go back and undo that day, so he would just have to live with it and take the time needed to heal.

Bessie didn't like Del's sullen mood and recognized the self-pity in which he was wallowing. She wasn't about to let him lie around being miserable and making everyone else miserable. As soon as he could get around a little bit she created odd jobs for him. He found doing everything one-handed was mighty difficult and he complained loudly about being so useless. Bessie ignored the complaining and kept him helping out in the kitchen as much as she could. After a few days of listening to complaints and excuses she set aside her cheerful attitude and quietly said she would not hear anymore complaining from him and he better get himself into the kitchen, now! Dumping a pan of dirty water into a bucket, Bessie told Del to carry it out and take care of it. Then she turned her back and began to sweep the floor without looking at him again.

Picking up the bucket Del quietly carried it outside, dumped it and set it under the pump. Pumping clean water into the bucket he swished it around, rinsed it out and threw the water to one side. No sooner had the water left the bucket and a group of cackling hens attacked the ground, scratching and scuttling about looking for food. Del went into the barn, scooped up some corn in his bucket and walked back out to the yard spreading the corn about the dry ground for the chickens. Cleaning out their water tray, he filled it with fresh water. His good arm leaning on the water pump, Del stood and watched the chickens drinking their water and contentedly pecking at the ground for food. A horse loudly whinnied, snorted and whinnied again. It was Del's pony inside the fenced yard by the barn. "Ah, there boy," Del softly spoke to him as he walked to the fence. The pinto whinnied again as he trotted smartly up close to the fence. Del rubbed the horse's face and neck. "You've missed me haven't you fella? I'm still here; still here fella." He got some fresh water for the pony and went searching for a brush. With his good hand, Del began brushing him down giving him needed attention.

The cool fall air was filled with the strong scent of horse, dry hay and grain. As he worked, Del became conscious of a gradual peaceful feeling taking over him and replacing the anger in his heart. The bitter disappointment left him; gratitude for his friends and the care and home they gave him moved deep inside. The rest of the day passed as Del moved about from one job to another. Bessie heard him whistling a tune as he washed up for supper and she knew he would be okay from now on.

It was a cold day that had started out with snow and wind. The family was taking refuge inside after the morning chores when much to Bessie's surprise, Del picked up her darning needle and started mending socks that she had thrown in a pile. When they were done, he found her extra pair of knitting needles and started knitting a new pair of socks. It was slow going as using both hands to knit was difficult. But, carefully, Del maneuvered the yarn and needles with determination and sure enough a new wool stocking began to take shape.

"Dang it, Del" Bessie remarked, "Your knitting looks better than mine in places!" She laughed out loud at the idea of a man out doing her knitting. She had new admiration for this young man who was resourceful enough to do just about anything for himself, even knitting.

Winter had come early this year and the family found themselves spending a lot of time inside the house. The boys became restless being cooped up with no way to spend their energy. Del, being a little restless himself, had fun entertaining them with stories and tall tales. He tried to come up with different games for them to play and one of his favorite board games was checkers. Finding an old checkerboard, Del looked for checkers but very few were found. Searching around the woodpile he picked out some small pieces of wood that could resemble game pieces. With much care and patience he showed the boys how to shave and sand them down. Spreading an old cloth over the table, Del had the boys touching them up with a little bit of paint found in the shed. The boys' faces showed serious determination as they eagerly worked on their pieces of wood and, before long, they had some real looking checkers. The glow of an oil lamp cast a bright golden light while adding a touch of warmth to the large room, as the boys spent many hours during the long cold evenings challenging each other.

Usually after the boys were tucked into bed, Del and Gaylord would sit about keeping the wood stove fed and talking about their thoughts and ideas of life in general.

"I'm considering giving up the homestead," Gaylord admitted one night. "The life here is good but Bessie and I have worked our hearts out trying to make this land yield. The droughts are bad and the cattle aren't thriving. But we've been saving up a little money, Bessie and me. When the time is right we plan to move on."

Troubled silence followed Gaylord's comments. The burning wood in the stove snapped and sizzled, the only sound to be heard other than an occasional gust of wind wailing outside the house. The room was dimly lit with just one small oil lamp on a table beside Bessie's chair as she worked on her knitting. Del's troubled eyes searched Gaylord's face with sincere concern, his stomach felt suddenly twisted in a knot. Del never dreamed that Gaylord and Bessie would ever be anywhere else other than right here. They had made a nice home for their family. They had made friends and gained a great deal of respect from the other homesteaders.

"It's true," Bessie joined in when she saw the look on Del's face. "Gaylord has found a place in British Columbia and he wants us to move there. It's a beautiful place in the mountains on a large lake. The railroad has just opened it up and will begin to sell off lots to make a town soon. Burns Lake, they call it. Can you imagine it?" Bessie said, putting her knitting in her lap, a far-off look on her face. "A land with trees and rocks, hills and a lake. I'm so tired of all this dust, dirt and flat land."

"British Columbia?" Del repeated. "Now just how far into British Columbia would that be?"

"Just west of Alberta, far beyond the prairie, deep into the Rockies where the forests are thick and tall and the mountains high. Everything will be brand new and the lots will be going cheap at first. With the money we've saved we want to open up a hardware store. No more farming, just a nice little store. We can get to know the folks and have things to sell that they will be a needin'. Should make a nice livin' that way."

Del leaned back in his chair; he grinned thoughtfully. "It won't be the same around here without you. Sounds like quite a plan," he said nodding his head and agreeing with the thought. He added with a big sigh, "Well, Gaylord, you will make a great business man."

Del laid in bed wide awake that night listening to the wind making soft whistles blowing about, demanding to be let in. He thought about what it would be like here without Gaylord and Bessie. He had seen other people moving on, working their lands and then leaving the homesteads, cattle and all. Memories of his journey with Clint, talking to the fur trappers from the big Northwest Territory crept into his head. The restless feeling for the mountains and a yearning for new places began to come to mind. But he had made a commitment and he conscientiously could not leave without finishing what he started. The land would not be his until he had settled it and worked it for three years. Then the government would give him title to his property. When he had signed those papers that was what he had set out to do. Work this land, build a farm and make a real home. Stubborn pride, if nothing else, would keep him here. Ah, but he would miss his good friends. "Maybe," he thought as sleep began to take over, "just maybe they would change their minds."

Stearns Homestead Cabin

# Chapter 21
## CERTIFICATE OF TITLE FOR THE LAND

By August 1915, Del had succeeded in fulfilling the requirements to claim his homestead. Gaylord Stearns and Fred Drafahl, as fellow homesteaders, filed a sworn statement to the Dominion Lands Agent in Oyen, a homestead inspector for the Calgary District, dated August 7, 1915. Their statements verified the work and development of Del's property. It took awhile for the paperwork to go through the proper channels, but by October 1915, Del was legally the proud owner of his 160-acre farm. The homestead files declared that Delbert Baxter, age 28 of Fair Acres, claimed a patent for a homestead under the provisions of the Dominion Lands Act for SE quarter of Section 24 Township 30 Range 4 W of 4th Meridian.

Completing the many questions listed on the papers, Del stated that he continuously lived on his homestead June 11, 1912 to December 17, 1913; March 12, 1914 to Nov. 1, 1914; and April 1, 1915 to August 1915.

They also required him to describe what developments had been made and the value of such. Thus, he furnished the description and value of his home and outbuildings as a 16' x 24' frame house, $500; a frame stable, $500; frame grain shed, $50.00; a well, $100 and pigs all fenced, $100.

According to his testimony, Del spent his first full winter on his homestead but he was not living on his homestead during the winter months of 1913-14 and 1914-15. This would be his logging time at Rocky Mountain House and the winter he spent recuperating at the Stearns home from his accident.

Finally, to complete his total requirements, Del also applied for and received his Certificate of Naturalization on June 6, 1915.

A Certificate of Title was granted from the Department of The Interior Land, Land Patents Branch, October 8, 1915 and was filed in Ottawa, May 1, 1916.

As Del worked and settled his homestead throughout those years the weather patterns gradually began to change over the great northwest. The land became dry and bleak. A great drought plagued the area. Time would show that the drought would last for several years. Many of the new farmers eventually gave up and deserted, leaving homes to turn into ghostly, wind torn shacks, and their barren lands to grow back to the empty rolling prairie grasslands. Only the very strong-minded would hang on, determined to ride out the destructive drought and hope for better days.

Del's fields and crops were not doing well, but his months at the logging camp provided him with enough money to get him by throughout the year. Hunting and fishing supplied him with plenty of food along with the vegetables that endured from the garden. Trapping now and then also brought in a bounty of furs. Because of his resourcefulness, Del seemed to live very well, while others struggled to survive.

During the winter of 1915-1916, Del spent another season at the great logging camp in Rocky Mountain House. Still working were many of the same men that had been there from his first trip, along with many new faces. Del settled in, worked hard and soon the cold winter days passed. With the arrival of spring, he was bound for home again.

Arriving home, the first thing that he did was check out his homestead, opening up the house and giving it a quick cleaning out. He then climbed on his pony and headed for Gaylord and Bessie's place.

It was Sunday and Del welcomed the familiar Sunday dinner of chicken and biscuits shared with Gaylord, Bessie and their family. Not much had changed in the area and any news over the winter Bessie had already shared with him through her many long letters. She never mentioned once during those letters about moving to British Columbia. Gaylord brought up the news; they were still making steadfast plans to leave their homestead and make a new home in Burns Lake, British Columbia.

Throughout that summer Del spent lots of time at the Stearns farm. The days of summer passed with the men helping each other with fieldwork and chores. Once the harvest was over, the family began to pack up their home and clean out the farm. The farm had been sold and they were ready to travel on.

The last of the trunks and boxes had been packed into the wagon. Most of the furniture had been sold except a few of Bessie's favorite pieces; blankets, quilts, dishes and clothes. All else would stay with the house. Their furniture was sparse and hand made; Gaylord promised new and better once they were settled.

The sun shone bright and warm the day Del drove them to the train station. Standing among the leather bags and wooden boxes of their belongings, they chatted for the last time. While filled with anxiety and sadness of leaving their old home and friends, Bessie and Gaylord couldn't help being overwhelmed by the anticipation and adventure of a new land filled with hope and promise. The train appeared in the distance, the smoke puffing and billowing black clouds into the air. Bessie turned to Del and gave him a strong hug as the tears suddenly streamed down her face. Del hugged her and patted her back softly, fighting his own tears. The train had arrived and people were boarding. As Bessie ushered Harry, Ralph, Fred, Grace and little Gaylord onto the train Del turned to Gaylord, looking him in the face. This man was his closest and dearest friend in the world. Gaylord grabbed Del's arm and shook his hand with a strong grip. "Thank you, Del. Thank you for everything." Del shook his head saying, "No, I thank you, I could not have survived here without your help."

As the family boarded the train they turned to wave goodbye one more time. Del raised his hand high and waved good-bye. His voice was filled with emotion as he exclaimed, "Good luck, be happy, be happy!" he repeated again more to himself as he slowly lowered his arm.

Del watched the train depart, the loud whistle blowing as it soon sped down the tracks moving far out of range, the train disappeared from site. Just like that, they were gone. Del turned and slowly left the station's platform. Climbing aboard the bare wagon, he sat down heavily. Mechanically, he urged the horses to move on. He felt drained and empty inside. The emotions he had denied himself all summer suddenly and forcefully besieged him. The Stearns family had really left; he was abandoned, deserted and so very alone. Somehow he knew deep down inside that he would never see this wonderful family again.

Stearns Family

71

# Chapter 22

## MAKING A CHOICE

Del had a few good weeks of trapping. After cleaning, stretching and drying the hides, they were ready to sell. The mid morning air had warmed somewhat, but a cool ceaseless wind let him know that summer had come to an end. Several fox, wolves and coyote furs covered the backside of his horse. Riding into town heading for the trading post his roan shied, snorted nervously and sidestepped off the trail as a small group of Northwest mounties rode toward him. Nodding his head, Del acknowledged them as they passed. The first mountie tipped his hat slightly while the others looked at him with curiosity then back to the path straight ahead. The mounties were beginning to be a familiar sight in the area.

Reaching the trading post, Del unloaded the furs. The small post was not much more than a rough built shack. With his arms full he unlatched the door pushing it wide open into a dim room. He turned, and with his foot, gave the door a shove and it slammed shut behind him. It took awhile for his eyes to adjust to the dimness after the bright sunlight outside. The air was heavy with the odor of musty decay mixed with tobacco smoke. A few other trappers had exchanged their pelts and were merely gathered about involved in deep conversation. All eyes turned to Del as a hush fell over the murky room. When they saw he was just a fellow trapper they muttered hellos and the conversation picked up where they had left off. As Del did his business with the buyer, he listened intently to the others. They were talking about the war and the many men who were dieing or severely wounded. Several of the local young men had been called away from their family and farms, duty-bound to join the army. The war, which was suppose to last only a few months, had dragged on and was getting worse.

It wasn't right, they were saying, Canada should not have to fight England's war, but they had no choice. The Prime Minister had gone against his word and was now enforcing the draft. Even the most secluded, remote lands of the Northwest Territories were not being overlooked. The Northwest mounties were sent to seek out to watch for men who had not signed up or who were avoiding their notice to report.

Taking the money from the trader, Del quietly walked outside without getting involved in the discussion. His life was filled with taking care of his animals, working his farm and hunting and fishing as he pleased. The outside civilization was far away and had nothing to do with him. He wanted to be left alone.

Del untied his horse and walked him down the street. The sky was clear and the day was bright. Some dust swirled about as gusts of wind blew through the streets and down through the small town. Lively children ran about, laughing and chasing each other down the boardwalk. A few buggies and a wagon rattled along the dirt street. A group of men were gathering at the livery stable getting ready for a horse auction. Not needing much for supplies, Del picked up his mail at the store. There was one lone letter in his mailbox and he quickly recognized the neat handwriting. Walking out onto the boardwalk he ripped open the envelope as he sat down on a worn wooden chair. All the commotion, noise, wind and dust, faded away as Bessie's words filled Del's mind.

*Dear Del,*

*Here we are, settled in at Burns Lake at last. It is early morning as I write, a strong cup of coffee sits by my side having brewed over the outside fire-pit. Gaylord has taken the boys into the woods to search for kindling and firewood. The pile near our tent is almost gone. Much to our surprise there are not many buildings here, yet. Most of the homes consist of large white tents, all laid out in long rows. There is a post office and a railroad station. The train stops three times a day dropping off the mail and supplies. There is a hotel going up, it's only half built right now. Gaylord has pitched in and is helping the men finish the building. When the people found out that we want to open a hardware store, the men offered to put up the building for us too. They are friendly, hardworking people that all look out for each other. Can you believe it? We are starting a new town, right from the very beginning. Green grass and large tall trees of every sort surround us. And the lake! It's a big lake surrounded by hills and mountains on all sides. Plenty of fish and wildlife survive here, supplying us with lots of good meals. Burns Lake is a most beautiful place. You could not find anything like it anywhere else on God's earth. The boys are happy here and have plenty to do to keep busy. A new schoolhouse is also in the plans for the town. God willing, our store and home will be finished before winter. We plan to live upstairs over the store. So, anytime you come to visit, you will have a place to stay. We all miss you and hope that you can come for a visit soon.*

*Love from all of us,*
*Bessie, Gaylord & children*

As Del finished the letter he looked out over the street and beyond to the open, flat prairie. He could vision Burns Lake, a different world far apart from Oyen, Alberta. It was good to hear from them and it sounded like they would do well. He was happy for Bessie and Gaylord. Maybe he would visit before winter. He folded the letter and put it in his shirt pocket mulling the thought over in his mind. He could travel west to see them before he went to Rocky Mountain House logging camp. That would be a good plan.

Del was suddenly hungry. It had been a long time since breakfast that morning. Down the street on the edge of town was a small café. Coffee and a hot meal would hold him over for the journey home. Sitting at a table by the window he was half way through the stew special when he saw two mounties ride up and hitch their horses to the rail. They looked around the small room as they walked in with a serious self important manner, then they took a table next to Del's. Del couldn't help overhearing their conversation as they waited for their meal.

"There's lots of places out there. Homesteaders throughout the countryside that we haven't checked on," one of the mounties was saying as he looked around the room. He made eye contact with Del and kept a steady gaze on him as he continued.

"We need to pay a visit to these farmers and find the men on this list. If they think they can hide out here on this desolate prairie land to avoid the draft, well, they have another think coming."

Del looked away and quickly finished his meal, quietly walked to the counter and paid his tab without being noticed. Once outside he turned his horse north and headed home hoping no one noticed which direction he went. During the twenty-mile ride the mounties' conversation kept going through his mind. He had signed up for his draft card when it became mandatory. Now he knew he would not be left alone. His time had run out. What would happen to his farm? There was nobody to take care of the cattle or horses. The neglected buildings would go to ruin. This war! The Canadian military would take him, put him in an army camp, send him overseas to lands far away to kill or be killed. Being told what to do, when and how to do it would be a life unbearable. It was not for him. This would not be serving his country. This was England's war, not Canada's nor the United States. A man should be able to make his own choice, not forced into being used as canon fodder for the British.

He had the money from the fur's he just exchanged. Adding that to the cash he had stashed away amounted to a good sum. It would be enough. His mind was settled, he now knew what he was going to do.

Back at the homestead Del moved about his house in automation, not giving himself time to think. He started packing all his belongings that he really wanted or needed to keep, stuffing them into leather saddle bags. Pots and pans hung on their hooks, tins on the shelf, and potatoes in the bin. The oil lamps remained on the table. A neat pile of wood pieces stacked in the corner by his chair in front of the window waited for whittling. Grabbing his canvass tarp and a few blankets from the bed he rolled them to fit on the back of his saddle. Outside he turned to the horses. Blaze would be the strongest and hardiest horse to ride for this trip. The big buckskin was tough as wet leather, with a thick black mane. Del had named him Blaze for the strip of white down his face. Del led him into the barn and quickly saddled and loaded him down. He knew this horse would be the best choice. Blaze would take him anywhere for as long as he needed. Lastly he thrust his rifle into its leather boot.    Walking to the pen he opened the gate and laid the poles on the ground. The pinto pony came to him searching for a treat. Nudging his arm she nickered lowly. Stroking the pony's head and mane Del looked at her with affection. The prettiest pony he had ever owned. She would be on her own now; back to the wild from where she had come. With a slap on the rump he gave a yell, "Yah – Yah! Go, go on now; you're free!" The pony jumped with surprise, then ran. The other horses followed and swiftly passed into the open fields, running without purpose, sheer instinct took them away from the homestead. Leaving the cattle was a different matter. They could survive on their own for awhile grazing on the prairie grass. Eventually, he knew they would wander over to a neighbor's farm and find a new home.

Del climbed into the saddle and swung the packed horse around, away from the setting sun. Riding to the top of the knoll he slowed, pulling the reins back around slightly. Raising his hat from his head he took one last look at his homestead. The wind had faded in the calm of the day's end and nothing moved, not even the tumbleweeds. The image would be embedded into his brain forever. The years of work; he had done well. It was a fine farm, and now it was time to move on. He had made his decision to go and he would not look back with regret. He turned Blaze around and rode on. Slipping off into the night, Del brought to a close another chapter in his young life.

# Chapter 23
## A Place in Montana

A small mountain stream trickled off a cliff side before it gurgled and rippled its way down through the rocks. Del filled up his water canteen and took a long drink of the cool refreshing water. Blaze also drank to his heart's content, moving downstream, following the flow until it merged with a good size creek. It was early morning; the sun was steadily rising above the horizon casting a warm glow about the gray sky. Del gave Blaze a much needed rest and fed him a little of the grain that he had brought with him. It had been three days' traveling since they had left the homestead.

Not far off there was a crossroads of sorts and some kind of small settlement; a flourmill beside the creek and a sawmill on the other side with a small wooden bridge between. The big doors of a blacksmith shop were wide open and Del could hear the sounds of someone working inside even though it was barely daylight. Walking closer, Del stopped and tied Blaze to a nearby tree. The bellows flared and pangs of metal against metal, along with the familiar smell of the leathers and hot irons, greeted him.

The smithy was not an old man, although his hair and beard were snowy white. Happy to see a stranger and curious about where he came from and where he was going, he greeted Del eagerly. Jake was his name, Jake Farrenton. He had a home just down the way, he told Del, pointing toward the other side of the road, two or three houses past a wooded thicket.

"There's coffee on the stove over there, help yourself." He was pleased for the company and hoped Del would stay and chat awhile. The time always went by faster when someone shared the tedious hours. Del was happy for the coffee; it was just what he needed to perk him up after riding all night. A few biscuits remained in a tin beside the stove. As Del eyed them, Jake read his mind.

"Take some biscuits too! The wife made them early this morning and I've had enough already."

Del sat down on a low stool wolfing down the biscuits and enjoying the coffee. "What's the name of this place?" he asked. "How far from the border would we be?"

"Sage Creek Crossing. That's what people here call this place. You're about forty miles from the Canadian border right here." Jake briefly wondered why Del needed to know this.

"Forty miles!" Del mumbled more to himself than out loud. Jake looked at him quizzically so he explained. "That means that I have ridden a total of eighty miles throughout the night. I was up near Medicine Hat, Alberta when I started out."

Del didn't say anymore out loud, but that little bit of information left Jake wondering what it was all about.

Del's tired mind wandered back to his last stop in Medicine Hat. He had planned to find a room with a bath and a good meal before moving any further. But – at a small hotel where he had chosen to stop, a Northwest mounty followed him into the lobby and was asking the clerk about directions. The mounty went on his way and the clerk smirked as he left. Turning to Del, he told him the mounties were searching everywhere for draft dodgers. "Combing the city clean," were his exact words. Del thanked the clerk for the information, deciding he wouldn't need a room after all and left. Thoughts of a soft bed and warm bath vanished quickly.

Jake's voice brought him back to the present. "That's a long haul for sure, especially night traveling!" He was hoping to learn more but Del was about done talking.

It felt good to rest; at last he could loosen up and relax without worry. Del appreciated Jake's good hospitality and enjoyed talking to him. But he was too tired to really be good company at the moment. Maybe it was the warm shop, the hot coffee and, finally, food in his stomach that made him not want to go any further.

"There wouldn't be any place around here that I could get a room?"

"There's a few rooms behind the mercantile", Jake said. "There are stables behind it, too. They will take care of your horse for you."

Del thanked Jake for the much appreciated coffee and biscuits and left to check out the rooms. He told Jake he would be back to see him after he got some rest. Jake went back to his work, shaking his head. "Riding all night long. That was fool crazy! What could that be all about," he wondered.

Del untied Blaze and led him down the dirt street. He had no thoughts of getting back on that horse at the moment. The walking felt good. It wasn't much of a town, but morning was bringing some people out as they started their way to work at the mill. The men looked at him with curiosity, most of them nodding a hello as they passed. It wasn't very often a stranger came to town, unless it was a friend or relative of someone they knew. He soon came to a square two-story building that had "Mercantile" painted across the front. The livery stable was very large. John Kelly had watched Del walk down the street and go into the store. He figured he would be bringing the horse in so he got a stall ready.

John met him at the door. "A quarter a night and we'll give him grain, water and clean bedding. I'll even brush him down for ya." He was happy to take care of Blaze and admired him openly. "I've got a clean box stall all ready for him right here."

John immediately started taking the saddle off Blaze. Del unloaded his rifle and saddlebags. All of his belongings, everything he owned in the world were here in these bags. It suddenly hit him what little he owned. A wave of sadness overtook him as he looked at his meager possessions. A few days ago he owned a whole farm, cattle, horses and a house filled with his own things. It was the weariness working on him. Tomorrow would bring a new day. He needed to rest.

John was a friendly boy and talked nonstop as he worked. His father owned the place, he explained. His ma and pa ran the store and he took care of the stables.

"It's a large place", Del commented. "Do you keep lots of horses here?"

"No, we sell and trade and sell a little feed and grain, too. But it's not like what it used to be." John replied. "It was before my day, but I've heard all the stories about 'back in the old days'. The place was built back when the fur trade was really big here. They took in lots of horses for the trappers. The trappers would come in to congregate at Sage Creek Crossing for the winter. They would wait for the spring thaw to flood the creek. With the high waters they put the skins on big rafts and floated down to Ft. Benton. But the beaver fur trade died out years ago and only an occasional trapper passes through now and then."

"Ft. Benton?" Del said, more as a question than a statement. "Is that far away?"

John had no idea how far it really was in miles. "It's a trip. About a two day ride by horse and wagon. Pa and I go down there once every month to buy supplies for the store. It's due south right on the Missouri.

It's a good size town. All kinds of people. We usually see Canadian mounties there, even. Pa says they buy provisions even though they are from Alberta. Must be the closest place to their post."

John's last remarks were all in innocent conversation. Del was startled to hear him talk about the mounties. It was almost as if he knew that's what Del was running from.

"Hmm. That's quite interesting." Del remarked as he gave John a quarter and picked up his bags and rifle. "I was just curious where it was."

His room at the back of the store was small and none too warm, but the large cot looked very inviting. It was mid-afternoon by the time Del woke up. There wasn't any kind of diner or café around, but he was able to buy some food at the store. There was still quite a bit of the afternoon left so he wandered back toward Jake's shop. Maybe Jake would know of a ranch where he could find work.

As he watched Jake work he admired his skill. He began telling Jake about the small blacksmith shop on his Pa's farm. They could do just about anything they needed to do there, for the farm. It wasn't long and the afternoon was almost gone. As the two men shared stories about their work, a young man appeared at the door, tall and slim with a crop of curly blonde hair.

"There's Joey! You come to town to have supper with us tonight? How you making out over there at Will's place?" Jake asked with genuine sincerity.

Joey glanced at Del. "This here is Del, came in early this morning, found a room over at the store." Jake explained.

Joey nodded his head at Del, shook hands with him then shoved both hands back into his pockets. Worried lines creased his forehead and his voice was filled with concern as he talked fast.

"I've got a problem with one of the horses. She quit eating yesterday, she's acting real nervous, she's down and then she's up, pacing around and then she's down again. And the big horse, Molly, got her leg caught in the barbwire and ripped it open pretty good. I got it cleaned up, sure did bleed a lot. She's limping pretty bad. Dam fences, horses weren't meant for barbed wire. Uncle Will needs to have just wooden fences around his barns."

Jake kept on working as he talked – "What ya know about horses, Joey? Did you ever have any before?"

"Nope, I can ride. Uncle Will taught me when I was a little kid. I used to come out here every summer. He taught me a lot about horses, but I've never had to take care of them when they was sick or hurt like this." He sighed long and hard – "I just don't know what to do? Uncle Will said the closest vet is Ft. Benton, that's a ways away."

Del couldn't help but wonder why this kid knew so little. He asked, "So where is Will now? Don't you have anybody to help you?"

"Nope, I'm stuck out there by myself, in that backwoods hole in the ground!" As Joey looked at Del his face told it all. The sad look of hopelessness fortified his statement.

Jake put down his tools and filled Del in on the boy's story.

"Joe is from Chicago, a city boy. He's been staying here with Will and Sara, his aunt and uncle, since this summer."

"And so where are they now?" Del asked.

"Aunt Sara got sickly and wanted to go back to Chicago to her sister's. She hates it out here anyway and Uncle Will thought maybe staying the winter back home would help her feel better. He couldn't leave without someone to take care of things, so they left me here to look after their homestead."

Suddenly the obvious struck Del. "This sick horse wouldn't be a mare foaling would it?" Jake chuckled out loud. "I was about to say just that, Del."

Joe looked puzzled, turning his head from Del to Jake and back. "What's foaling?"

The two men laughed good-naturedly. Jake replied. "I think when you get back to that farm you might just have a new colt in there with that mare."

"Oh!" Joey's eyes got big. "So that's it! Oh my gosh! What do I do? Should I get the vet?"

"I know a little about horses. I can go with you and check her out if you'd like." Del offered. "If this is what it is, and it sure sounds like it, then these things usually just take their natural course. But it's always good to be prepared if the mare needs help. How far away are you?"

Joey didn't know Del at all but his friendly laugh and kind smile led him to believe that this stranger could be a friend. And, right now he sure needed a friend. Jake started to put his tools away and told them to go on ahead. He wanted to stop at his house and let his wife, Martha, know where he was going to be, then he would follow.

Jake watched the two of them leave. Del wasn't that much older than Joe but he seemed wise beyond his years. Strange how he just wandered in here, not saying where he was going or where he came from, riding through the whole night. He must have wanted to cross that border for a reason. Shaking his head he went about closing up the shop. There was a mystery here for sure; maybe Del would talk about it in time.

Del and Joe rode side by side on their horses as Joe talked about the land and different places as they passed them by. They moved at a quick pace along an open trail for about two miles before coming to the homestead.

The mare was lying down in the barn stall when they arrived. One quick look and Del knew she was in labor. Slowly, quietly they entered her stall. The mare was content with Joe in the stall with her and she made no notice of Del at all.

"Jesse, that's her name." Joey touched her face and talked to her reassuringly.

"Look, the colt is coming." Del told Joey.

"What's that?"

"It's the feet."

Joey could make out the tiniest tips of feet, suddenly with a groan and a shudder more of the feet appeared.

"See, there's the nose, the foal is coming just as it should." The front legs and the head appeared and the mare seemed to rest before giving another shudder and the whole colt slide out onto the straw covered floor. "Good girl!" Joey whispered as he stroked the horse's neck. "Good girl!" The horse nickered and laid her head down; Joey was alarmed , "what's wrong?"

"She's resting, she's okay. Let her be. Leave the mare with her foal, she will take care of him." Del said as he slowly left the stall, so as not to disturb the mare.

"Him? It's a him?"

"Yes", Del laughed, "The colt is 'a him'."

They watched from outside of the stall as the colt began to move about struggling. Jesse began nudging her baby and cleaning him off. Soon the colt was standing on wobbly legs looking for his first meal from his mother.

Joe was awe struck. He had never seen the birth of any kind before and it was the most fascinating event of his life.

"I can't believe it," he kept saying, "We just had a baby!"

Jake came in just in time to see the colt struggle to stand and nurse.

"Ahh, he is a beauty!"

Joe couldn't take his eyes off the mare with her colt.

"We have a baby!" he said again laughing, "And here I thought she ate something that made her sick!"

Together the three men checked out the other mare, Molly. The leg did have a nasty wound. "Joe had done a good job of cleaning it out," Del thought, as he examined the wound. "It could use a few stitches, but there's no need to fetch a vet. I can stitch it up for you." Joe and Jake both looked at Del with surprise. He sure sounded confident that he knew what he was talking about. Joe was nervous. He wasn't so sure he should let anybody fool around with Uncle Will's horse. "I don't know about that. What do you think Jake?"

Jake looked at Joe, knowing his concern. He shrugged his shoulders. "Why not try it? Do you think you could find some needles and thread?" Joe ran to the house and searched his aunt's sewing materials and found a heavy-duty needle and strong thread. Molly was a gentle horse and while Del swiftly did his work, Jake and Joe talked to her and kept her calm. This wasn't the first time that Del had sewn up an animal's wound. His knowledge and skill were evident to the other two men.

"The wound will have to be kept clean and tended to every day for a while. A few drops of Lysol in warm water will do it."

With both horses taken care of, their work there was finished. Jake said that he had stopped to tell Martha what was going on and that he would be back with Joe and Del for supper. The three of them were really hungry by this time and a home cooked meal sounded good. Jake and Martha didn't treat Del like a stranger. They warmly welcomed him into their home the same as they did Joe. Joe often took meals with them. Will and Sara were their good friends, so they had gladly agreed to watch out for Joe when Will and Sara had left for Chicago. Although Joe was a grown man of twenty years old, he was a city boy and very naive about country ways.

Del enjoyed the evening, and felt like he had known these folks all his life. An evening with Jake, Martha and Joe was a welcome change for him. He hadn't enjoyed time with a family like this since Gaylord and Bessie had left for British Columbia. He didn't realize how much he missed it. He was comfortable and relaxed. He soon opened up and began telling stories of his homestead and logging days.

Soon, and without thinking, he had confided in his new friends about his decision to leave his homestead and Canada before he could be drafted.

Jake sat back in his chair and listened as Del told of his recent decision because of the war.

So, thought Jake, this is what he was running from. "Well, he said with feeling, I don't blame you Del. This war is a terrible thing. I have a feeling that it won't be long and the States will be dragged into it, too. I can't find fault with a man for not wanting to be forced to fight a war like this one."

Del looked around the table at Jake, Martha and Joe as he talked. They each watched him with concern. "The fact is" Del went on, "It was time for me to go." He sat back in his chair, crossed his arms, talking in a slow serious manner. "I had lost my feeling for the place; there didn't seem much reason to stay. My brother went back home, my friends had sold out and moved on to British Columbia, and the drought was sucking the life out of the land."

Joe was quite taken up with Del. He admired his gumption and courage. How he wished he had that type of self-confidence to just go out on his own, with no destiny in sight, depending on only oneself for the next meal wherever it might come from.

"So, now what?" he asked. "Where do you go from here?"

"Del looked at Joe and didn't answer right away. "Well," he said, with a soft chuckle and slow grin. "that's one thing I'm not sure of yet. But, I'm working on it."

"I can't pay you anything," Joe blurted out, "but I can give you room and board. I sure could use some help, especially until Molly is healed up good. I'm not much for tending to things like that. Hell, I'm not much good at anything!" He laughed and they all laughed with him.

It didn't take Del long to consider the idea. He could stay there at the farm with Joe and help him take care of things until his uncle returned. Room and board would be enough for now.

Del welcomed this idea. He liked Joe and he needed a place to stay for awhile. He could live here and work things out in his mind as to what he was going to do and where to go from here. During his long night journey, thoughts of going back home had entered his mind. But he wasn't really ready to do that, not yet.

As they arrived back at the homestead, the sun had begun to set, making the buildings appear like silhouettes against a fading blue sky streaked with red. Uncle Will had a nice large well kept home, painted bright white with deep green shutters. A porch surrounded the house on three sides. Wild rose bushes, thick and full grew on each side of the porch steps. The barn is what Del admired the most, a large red barn with a mansard roof. A short steeple on the front had a tall iron-lightening rod. An ornate iron pole with a trotting horse on top of a copper arrow showed which way the wind was blowing.

"That's quite a weather vane; I've never seen one like it."

"Jake made that for Uncle Will at his shop. He makes lots of stuff like that." Creaking and groaning a very tall windmill stood near the barn waiting for the wind to power its mighty propeller. A typical homestead, there were no neighbors close by.

In the early morning Del was out checking on Molly's wound. He put a few drops of Lysol in a pan of water and cleaned it off thoroughly. It looked like it was going to heal nicely. A sleepy Joe wandered in when Del was cleaning out the horse stalls and spreading new straw. The new colt frolicked around his pen making tiny noises sounding a lot like a muffled whinny.

"You going to give this little fella a name?" He asked Joe. Considering the fact that it would be awhile before Uncle Will returned, Joe thought maybe he should do just that. "Shadow", he said without second thought. "He's pure black as night, just like a shadow. It fits." "It does fit," thought Del. He liked the name, so the colt was called Shadow from that day on.

Together they finished up the chores. Joe milked the only milking cow and then turned her out to pasture with the other beef cattle. Del fed the chickens and gathered the eggs while Joe fed the pigs. The pigs were fenced in behind the granary where they had access to going outside or in where they could stay sheltered. Grunting and squealing they ran toward the gate looking for their daily feed of slop and grain. Joe had a name for each of them and talked to them as he filled the feed and water troughs. "Morning Pinky, Brownie, Spottie! Don't be selfish now, ya got to share."

"I just love these guys, Del. Ain't they the cutest critters."

Del had been raising pigs all his life and try as he might, he could not find anything cute about hogs. He watched Joe as he leaned over the fence watching the pigs gulp in as much slop as they could get, pushing and nudging their way down the trough. Their long dirty snouts and fat short bodies gave off a terrible stench from the mud they wallowed in.

"The only thing cute about pigs is when they're cooking in the oven."

"Cooking in the oven?" Joe hadn't really given much thought to what happens to pigs. "Ah ha, sure, cooking in the oven." he repeated, stepping back off the gate railing. With that thought, Joe was sure he would never be able to eat pork again.

It was time for breakfast and Joe said he would fix them up some eggs. Del soon discovered that fixing eggs was about all that Joe knew how to do in the kitchen. And that included washing the dishes. Dirty pots, pans and plates were piled on top of the dry sink and strewn about on the table. Joe was a little embarrassed about the messy kitchen and he tried to make light of it.

"I really should have more dishes. I use them, and when I need them they are dirty, then what do you do?"

With a chuckle Del replied, "Ya, seems to me, a few more dishes is just what you need. Let's get a few buckets of water and see what we can do with this mess."

Filling a large pan with the well water, Del sat it on the wood stove to heat for washing dishes. He went about making some coffee and offered to make home fries if Joe could find some potatoes. As Joe fetched the potatoes from a bin in the cellar he knew he was going to enjoy Del being here. Cooking was something he never bothered to learn and now they could have some good grub.

Joe poured the fresh milk into a big glass jug and what they didn't use for breakfast he sat on a shelf inside the pantry, where it would stay cool.

Del couldn't resist making up a batch of buttermilk biscuits. While looking for flour and other ingredients, he found a small wooden butter churn stored in the corner of the pantry. "Did you ever make butter, Joe? We must have plenty of milk here for just the two of us; we could easily make up some butter with the churn."

"Butter?" Joe looked up from washing the last of the pots. "No, I never made it myself. Aunt Sara has some stored in a glass jar there inside the pantry. There's some left, I'm sure."

Pouring the milk in a long shallow pan Del set it to one side on the broadshelf, covering it with a large flat tin cover.

"Now in the morning we will skim off a cup or two of the cream. After a few days, we'll have enough cream and we can churn up some butter." It would help pass away the long winter hours and they would end up with good home fresh butter.

Joe paid attention with interest. He was quick to watch everything Del did from making coffee, baking biscuits, to cooking up the best home fries. Never had he seen any man in his family cooking and cleaning. That was women's work. He couldn't quite imagine his mother even letting him get close to "her" kitchen, let alone actually cook something. But, if a man like Del could do all of this, as well as he does, then it was something worth learning. Besides, who knows how long Del will stay around?

Early evening arrived with a brisk cool wind. The kitchen was clean, the chores were done, wood had been chopped to fit into the wood stoves and the wood boxes in the kitchen and parlor were filled. Del and Joe settled inside relaxing with a good warm fire going in the parlor stove. Del found a drawing half finished lying on the lamp table. It was a sketch of the farm with the horses standing inside the corral. As he picked it up to admire it, he found many other sketches underneath it. It was then, looking around the room, that he noticed many, many drawings scattered about. One was a lady sitting in a rocking chair, knitting. Aunt Sara he presumed. Another was a farmer standing beside Jesse, the horse, bridle in hand. That had to be Uncle Will. Looking from the pictures to Joe he said. "Did you draw these?"

"Ya," Joey said as he sprawled out on a large wooden rocking chair, one leg draped over the arm. He automatically rocked as he talked. "I like to draw and it helps to pass away the time. All of these are mine" he said as he spread his arm about the room.

Del walked around surprised at how good each of them was. On the piano top was a particularly nice one framed of a very pretty young girl. Dark sparkling eyes seemed to dance peering straight into his own eyes. "Pretty girl!" he remarked not taking his eyes off the picture.

"That's Emma. My Emma. She's the reason I'm here." Del sat the picture back in its place and sat down in a large padded chair beside Joe. Knowing there was a story here he didn't say anything and waited for Joe to continue.

"Emma's the sweetest little thing you could ever know. A tiny gal with long dark hair that shimmers with a touch of red in the sunlight. She's got spunk and laughter in her voice all the time. Emma just has to look at me with that little perky look and her smile makes me melt. We grew up together; she's my best friend. Her folks are poor and have lots of kids. Her father is a caretaker for one of our neighbors and her mother takes in washing for people. They live in a small caretaker's cottage behind our neighbor's big house. I love my Emma and she loves me, but my folks don't think she is good enough. They say we are too young and they've tried everything to keep us apart. They sent me out here so I would forget about her." Joe quit rocking and moved about the room, stopping to stare out the window into the night darkness.

"It didn't work." He continued. "I think about Emma every day. Evenings like this, I wonder where she is and what she's doing. I broke her heart when I told her I was leaving. She cried and carried on something awful. She wanted to come with me. She thought we could get married and be together forever." Joe turned and sat down again, his elbows on his knees, head in his hands facing Del. "The fact is, I don't know how to take care of her. I mean, if we got married and stayed together, what would I do? My parents wouldn't let us stay with them. I didn't have a job that paid anything. I didn't have any answers for her. I really let her down."

After a short pause he added, " And that's why I'm here!"

Del let out a long sigh. He wasn't sure what to say. He felt sorry for Joe. Too young to know what he was really doing, he had a lot of growing up left to do. Del absentmindly picked up some small pieces from the wood box and with his pocketknife began whittling. For a few moments complete silence filled the room. A burning piece of wood sizzled and snapped inside the potbellied stove. The mantle clock struck softly seven times announcing the hour. Del started talking to Joe without looking at him.

"I've been in your shoes before, Joe. I met this little gal and just couldn't stay away from her. It didn't matter what anyone told me, I wouldn't listen. And lots of folks made it their business to tell me she was too young, not the girl for me. I was so love sick I couldn't hear what they were saying."

When he didn't say anymore, Joe looked at him hunching his shoulders with a quizzical look.

"So, what happened? What did you do? "

Del kept his eyes on his work and never once quit whittling.

"I married her."

Surprised, Joe sat up straight then slowly leaned back in his chair.

"You married her?"

"Yup, I married her. I bought a nice little farm, brought her there and settled right in." Del turned his piece of wood examined it closely then continued to whittle before saying more.

"It was less than a year and she was tired of it. Tired of the farm, tired of being married, tired of me. More than anything I couldn't stand to hear everyone saying, ' I told you so'. I sold the farm to my brother. Got on a train and headed west without a plan or a thought in my head as to where I was going or what I was going to do."

"And," he paused looking up at Joe, "That's why I'm here!"

With that they both laughed out loud, breaking the gloomy mood.

"Women!" Joe shouted, throwing up his hands toward the ceiling. "What do we do with them and what do we do without them!"

# Chapter 24
## HUNTING COYOTES

As the days passed, winter moved closer. Del taught Joe how to do numerous things around the farm, including cooking more than just eggs. He often wondered how Uncle Will ever expected this kid to survive! Must be he figured he would either sink or swim.

Del had been searching through the barn and found an old buggy in bad need of repair stored on the other side of the hayloft. New wheels plus a few other replacement parts might make it serviceable again.

Joe finished laying new bedding in the calf pens then worked his way to the back of the barn. "What ya looking for Del? Not much back here except old wagons and a buggy."

"Well," replied Del, "I've looked all over this place and I haven't seen a sled or a sleigh. Its been spitting snow off and on now for a few days and we aren't going to be able to get around very well with Uncle Will's big buggy. Not even a wagon will work in deep snow. What did he use?"

"Oh, that's right! I'd forgotten all about that. Uncle Will's old sleigh was in real bad shape. He banged it up last winter and made it worse than ever before. He smashed it into some rocks and busted up one runner. Instead of fixing it up he gave it to one of the new neighbors. They were just starting out last year homesteading and needed one real bad. The fella said he could fix it good enough to use. Uncle Will figured he would buy a new one this summer before winter set in. I'm sure he never thought about it at the time he and Aunt Sara left for Chicago. Damn! What do we do now?"

Joe stood with his hands in his pockets, raised eyebrows and a blank look on his face. Del couldn't help but laugh a little at his helplessness.

Slowly Del walked around the old buggy and studied it closer.

"Well, my boy, I think maybe we can take this here old buggy and make it into a sleigh. We'll have to go into town to that lumber mill and buy some wood to fix it up. Mark my words, it's going to do just fine."

It was early in the morning with lots of daylight left. Using the wagon, they rode into town. They hadn't gone far when Del pulled the team of horses to a standstill. Joe followed Del's gaze as he turned around looking out over the countryside. All was still; no birds or jabbering squirrels could be heard. Then Joe heard what Del was listening for, a long low howl, followed by another and then another.

"Wolf! Del, that's a wolf we hear."

"Ah huh, more than one of them out there. We gotta get that sleigh built soon. I got a hunch that we will be needin' it for hunting some wolves!"

"Oh, ya? Wolf hunting, that's something I've never done before!"

"You don't say!" Del looked at Joe with mock surprise. "I better give you some shooting lessons soon."

After buying the needed wood, they went to visit Jake at the blacksmith shop to get some brackets and metal strips for the runners. Jake was pleasantly surprised as Joe excitedly told him about their plans to go hunting wolves.

"Good idea! Ya know, Del, there is a good bounty on those wolves. They've been after the homesteaders' cattle and sheep, a real bad nuisance. Not only the wolves," he added as an afterthought, "but there are packs of coyotes out there, too."

"You boys going to come over to the house and have some supper with us tonight?"

Del worked it over in his mind a little bit, thinking about Martha's good cooking. He knew Joe was ready to jump at the chance of getting out of cleaning up dishes.

"We really should get back. I've got to get that sleigh done soon."

"Ah, come on Del. You've got lots of time to fix up that old buggy into a sleigh. It's not going to snow for weeks yet." Joe was ready to stay, crossing his arms he sat down on the stool, determination set on his face. Jake didn't help much. "Martha was baking pies yesterday. I think there's an apple and one mincemeat left on the pantry shelf."

That's all it took to make Del give in. "Okay, but we have to get back early. And no shooting lessons until this sleigh is done."

The next day Del and Joe pulled out the old buggy, stripped off the wheels and replaced them with runners. With the sleigh finished, they were ready for shooting lessons.

"Place the rifle firmly against the right shoulder. Look through the site, line up the target, and slowly squeeze the trigger. You pull that trigger too quickly, the rifle kicks and your bullet goes astray. When you find your prey you've got one shot, one chance." Del explained as Joe carefully handled the rifle.

The sudden power that burst in Joe's hands as the rifle fired surprised him. The rifle hit his shoulder knocking him back and he looked up stunned. All of the tin cans still remained sitting on top of the fence posts. Again, slowly, he placed the rifle back firmly against his shoulder, closing one eye to better see the target through the site with the other eye, finger tense on the trigger, slowly, slowly he squeezed, preparing himself for the force; the rifle went off with a blast and a can flew off the post high into the air.

"I hit it!" He yelled, "I hit it! Whoopee!"

Raising the rifle into the air he danced in a circle while he whooped. Running and jumping through the field he found the can and picked it up to examine the hole. They spent hours setting up targets to shoot at for the rest of the afternoon. Eventually, they moved them further away and used different sizes. It was a great sport and Del was enjoying teaching it to Joe.

After that, each morning Joe eagerly worked on the chores so that he could practice target shooting.

"I'm ready for a hunt. I want to do this." He insisted one evening. Del and Joe sat at the table, cleaning their rifles by the light of a lantern. Darkness had come early; the air was still and cold.

"Okay, we'll go. I haven't been too far about these parts. We'll have to do some scouting around first. First thing tomorrow we'll head out." Del put his gun onto the homemade gun rack on the wall and mounted the one Joe had borrowed from Uncle Will's collection right under it. Picking up the gun oil and cleaning cloths, he turned out the lantern and stoked up the wood fire.

"We'll get up early tomorrow. We better hit the hay." Del was more than ready for this hunt and he finally felt confident enough that Joe was ready too.

The following day Del and Joe were up just before sunrise to do the chores. During the early morning hours the sun came up in a cold cloudless blue sky. Not a breath of air was stirring.

Del stood peering into the small mirror on the wall above the wooden washstand. He just finished washing up and shaving. Wiping his hands on the cotton towel he gave it a twirl along the wooden dowel that held it to the side of the stand. Joe was making a lot of racket in the kitchen. He was attempting to put together some flapjacks for breakfast. Suddenly a strong wind came up whistling and clamoring about the house. A loose shutter began to pound loudly against a windowpane. Del opened the back door to throw out the water from the washbowl and he could see the windmill churning furiously about. A very dark cloud loomed overhead. A few scattered snowflakes began to swirl about. Del feared a fast incoming blizzard. Finding the guilty shutter he hinged it back before it could break the window, then ran to the barn to find a hammer to fix the loose latch on the shutter. Looking around the horse barn he found a good strong piece of rope. Hoping it would be long enough, he tied one end of it to a large ring on the outside of the barn and ran it straight across the yard to the house. It just barely reached the edge of the porch where it could be tied to another large ring. "Perfect," Del thought. This is exactly what the rope was meant for. He hammered the loose shutter latch and pounded a few more of the others just for good measure. The temperature was dropping drastically and the snow began to fall heavily, quickly covering the ground.

Joe had come out onto the porch watching him.

"What's the rope for?"

"You'll soon see. We better make sure everything is latched down tight and get back inside. Hurry!"

Del and Joe ran around the yard chasing the chickens into their coop and latched the door tight. They picked up everything lying around the yard, (a small wheelbarrow, rakes, hay forks) and put them in the barn. Joe gathered up a few glass tumblers and coffee mugs that had carelessly been left on the porch. A tablecloth from the porch table began to blow away. With his hands full, Joe did a quick juggling act and caught it just as it lifted into the air. Frozen snow pelting hard, mercilessly stinging his face.

"Whoa," said Joe, catching his breath, "this is going to be a bad one."

By the time they got back into the house they couldn't see their hands in front of their faces. They were both freezing from the bitter cold. Huddling by the kitchen wood stove they warmed their freezing fingers and toes.

The oil lamp, with its soft glow, cast shadows about the room. The storm howled outside slamming against the buildings while inside they were warm and snug. They had put off as long as possible going back outside, but the animals had to be tended to. They couldn't neglect them any longer.

"Keep close to that rope and follow it to the barn," Del explained pulling on boots and buttoning up his coat tight to his neck. "The wool hat is not going to be enough. Here, you need to wrap this scarf over your face too."

Once outside even the rope was invisible. Slowly Del and Joe went step-by-step trudging in deep snow. With heads down, they pushed against an invisible force that stole their breath and whipped their eyes. With numbed fingers, they held fast to the rope guiding the way to the barn.

Once inside, Joe didn't want to return.

"Thank God, Del, you knew enough to hang up that rope. What would I have done here alone?"

Finally, they hunkered down for a long night. The blizzard continued all through the dark hours piling the snow over the countryside, leaving drifts as high as the windows.

The land, trees and rooftops covered in white, glimmered in the calm morning sunshine. In the quiet aftermath of the storm, tiny winter birds could be heard chirping from the bushes.

Del nimbly climbed out of the window onto the porch. Luckily they found a shovel in the woodshed at the back of the house. Bitter air bit sharply into his skin as he moved to the outside, away from the warmth of the wood-burning stove. The snow was heavy, but it didn't take him long to shovel out the blocked entrance to the kitchen. After shoveling a path to the barn, they checked on the animals. Frosted breath escaped from the horses as they sighed a greeting, eagerly waiting for food. The barn was not much for warmth, but at least they were sheltered and safe.

"I'm worried about those beef cattle, Joe. If the drifts are very bad out there in the fields, they might not be able to move into the shelter and get food. We've got to ride out there and bring them back in. There's only about fifteen of them and plenty of room in the barn."

The horses struggled through the drifts and on down the fields. A rough lean-to had been built to give the cattle some shelter and extra feed. They found the cows all huddled together, their food supply gone. Herding them along toward the barn seemed to be an endless job. The cows weren't happy to be moving away from their shelter and needed constant prodding. Finally, with the cows safely inside the barn, they could think about hunting.

While out in the fields they could see many signs of the wolves. All around them, tiny footprints were imprinted in the new fallen snow. They were too small for the cattle to make and just the right size for wolves or coyotes.

Molly's leg was well healed by now, so Del hitched her up to the sleigh. Joe saddled up Jessie and rode her out along the fields beside Del's sleigh. It was getting on toward evening when they came across a coyote. Del started circling around him with the sleigh. Joe, following Del's instructions, took after the coyote. The stalked animal didn't know which way to run with the horse and sleigh speeding around him. Joe stopped, aimed and fired. He had shot his first prey. They repeated the same tactics as they came across more and more of the wild animals. Sometimes they were alone and sometimes they were in small packs.

Del and Joe arrived back at the farmhouse after the first big hunt, encouraged by their good luck. The sleigh was loaded down with coyotes. Now, the job of skinning and stretching the hides was another lesson for Joe to learn. As the winter passed, the number of coyote hides hanging up in the barn increased.

The worst of the winter was over when Joe received a letter from Uncle

Will and Aunt Sara. They would be returning to their farm in about two weeks' time. Uncle Will was anxious to get back before the spring work was needed to be done. Even Aunt Sara, feeling stronger now, was lonesome for her home and to see her own things about her.

During a trip into Sage Creek Crossing, Del paid a visit to the stables. John had just the right little horse that would work out well for a packhorse. He gave him a fair price as the horse had been there awhile. Inside the office, John wrote him up a bill of sale.

"Where would the closest place be for trading in furs around here?" Del inquired.

John put away his books and thought about it for a moment.

"Well, I suppose Ft. Benton is the only place about these parts. Nothing else that I know of."

He started to tell where it was located. Del interrupted. "I remember, you told me once. It's down on the Missouri." Del was also remembering that John had told him the Northwest mounties frequently visited Ft. Benton.

"That's the only place, huh? What about east of here?"

"Don't know for sure. I think you'd have to go a long ways. Check with Pa inside the store, he might have a better idea."

Del didn't check with John's pa. Instead he walked his new horse over to Jake's shop. He needed some shoes on the horse anyway before he took off for too far away.

Jake put aside his other work and went right to work on shoeing the horse. He told Del he was sorry to hear he was planning to leave.

"You've done lots of good for Joey, made a real cowboy out of that fella. His uncle certainly will be surprised when he gets back here. Still no special plans on where you're headed?"

"Nope, nothing for certain. If I don't find work on a ranch I might just head back up north and build a good trap line. Like to see what I can do. There's good money in it."

"Ya," Jake agreed. "But, you've got to live in that wilderness, can get mighty tuff." Jake shook his head with concern.

"Yes, siree, I guess it might be." Del tossed this about in his mind then clearly said, "But then that's the fun of it!" He chuckled while trying to keep the horse calm as Jake worked on him. Holding the horses halter, he patted his neck. He was happy with this little horse; he had a feeling that he'd work out good for him. "Ginger," he thought to himself. "Ginger would be a good name."

"Joe and I ended up with a good lot of coyote hides. Never did find those wolves. I intend to turn them in and send Joe his share of the money. Where's the best trading post?"

"Ft. Benton." Jake said without hesitation.

"Hmm, so I've heard. Nothing else around?"

"Na, that's it. You'd be crazy to try to go any further. Ft. Benton is far enough as it is."

Paying Jake for his work, Del shook hands and bid him goodbye. Jake stood in the doorway of his blacksmith shop and watched him leave.

"If I come back this way, I'll be sure to stop by and say hello. Give my best to Martha. I will never forget her pies!" Del called out as he turned and trotted off with his new packhorse in tow.

A week later Del started getting his gear and possessions together.

"I've got something for ya, Del."

Del looked up from packing his clothes into the saddlebags. Joe stood in the doorway holding out a couple sheets of drawing paper.

"Maybe it's something you will remember me by." On one paper was a sketch of Del sitting on a wagon, rifle in hand, shooting. The other was Del sitting on Blaze, hat back far on his head, looking away, as if searching for his next destination.

Del took the drawings, carefully looking them over. "You sure are a good artist, Joe," he said as he rolled the papers up with care and tucked them into the bags.

Joe stood, hands in his pockets, eyes on the floor. He didn't say much of anything, just a plain "Thank you."

"It's been good being able to stay the winter here, Joe, but I've got to move on and start searching for a job somewhere. I'm getting mighty restless and anxious to explore what's ahead and find real work. Something that pays money!" Del added with a chuckle.

With everything else ready, Joe helped Del pile the dried coyote skins onto the packhorse.

"I'll send you your share of the money from the hides as soon as I get them traded down at Ft. Benton."

"And where will you go from there, Del?"

"Not sure yet. There's a place I've heard about far north in the Canadian Rockies; it's called Peace River Country. There's some good huntin' and trappin' to be done there. I might try it out."

It was not easy to say good-bye; they had become good friends. Del had come to think of Joe as a younger brother. Knowing he probably would not ever see him again, he hoped he would do well with his life. He turned to Joe and shook his hand with a tight grip.

"You just might become a farmer yet, Joe. Ya know, maybe you should head back to Chicago and find that little gal you've been pining over. She won't stay waitin' too long."

"I'll be off now, but mark my words; you'll be getting some money in the mail."

Del slipped easy onto Blaze's saddle then picked up the lead rope to Ginger, the little packhorse. No more words were said. As Blaze turned down the path leading out of the farmyard, Del turned toward Joe once more and waved good-bye.

Joe stood there in front of the barn looking small, with both hands in his pockets, a lot like the first time they had met. He waved back and didn't move from that spot until Del was well out of sight.

# Chapter 25

## CHARLIE

Del wandered down the trail going further into Montana toward the Missouri River and Ft. Benton. It was getting toward nightfall when he came upon a peddler's wagon pulled into the woods just off the road a ways. The peddler had set up camp for the night. Climbing down from Blaze, he walked carefully toward the wagon and the campfire the peddler was building. Looking up in surprise as Del approached, the old peddler offered a friendly "good day to ya", and a short nod of his head, as he stood up looking somewhat leery. Hoping to reassure the peddler that he was not going to rob him or do him harm, Del put out his hand to shake. After explaining that he was headed toward Ft. Benton to trade his furs and looking for directions, the old man loosened up and offered him some coffee. It wasn't long before Del was settling in to share the campsite for the night. Together they shared their provisions and cooked some supper over the open fire. The next morning, bright sunrise shown over the horizon as the old peddler pulled out to travel east. Del moved further west. The peddler had told him he didn't have much further to go; the trading post was this side of Ft. Benton. Possibly he wouldn't have to enter the town at all.

As it turned out, his "not much farther" was another whole day's ride. Del came upon the ranch at almost sunset. The place was large and served as a boarding house as well as the trading post. Many horses filled the corral. The trader was a heavy, sweaty man with long tangled dark hair mixed with gray. When he smiled, his teeth were yellowed with big gaps between them. Del hesitated when the trader offered him some supper and a room at the boarding house, but he was tired and if he left he would soon have to make camp somewhere. He decided to take the room even though his gut feeling was to leave and move on. As he paid for the room this feeling of dread did not leave him. He took his horses to the barn and a couple of men came in and said they would take care of them. Del watched as they pushed his horses in with the lot of very large horses.

Taking his saddlebags he walked on into the boarding house. Although the building was large it was dark and dimly lit. Frayed curtains hung at the windows and old musty smelling furniture furnished the room. After a decent supper of beefsteak and fried potatoes he was shown his room. Again the smell of old tobacco and musk filled the room. A large bed along with a small table and a short chest of drawers was all that the room held. A dingy shade pulled all the way down covered the only curtainless window. The floorboards held a dull, faded rug. At least it would make the floor a bit warmer, Del thought as he got ready for bed. After Del turned off the oil lamp he pulled up the shade and looked out over the barnyard. A bright moon lit up the night. He could see his poor horses squashed among the big horses of the corral. Blaze and Ginger were good size horses but they looked very small and frightened. Again he wished he hadn't stayed here for the night.

He slept fitfully through the night. While getting dressed the next morning, he thought he would have slept better on the cold ground under some trees out in the woods. He went to fetch his horses, leaving this place far behind couldn't be soon enough. A young man was on his way out the door at the same time. They both headed for the barn. The fellow was a tall man, lean, reddish brown hair and seemed about the same age as Del. The tall man nodded to Del and said "cheers" with a strange accent.

"Name's Charlie". He shook Del's hand and quickly let go, scratching his head and then his arms and chest.

"Del, Del Baxter". Watching Charlie itch made Del itch too. The more he scratched the more he itched, his arms, his legs and mostly his head. They walked to the barn this way chatting as they went and each of them scratching as hard as he could. Charlie looked at Del and surmised, "This bloomin place is lousy! I never itched so bad me whole life!"

"Lousy!" It finally sunk in to Del what all the itching was about. "Lice! I didn't sleep much all night, now I know why. I knew I shouldn't have stayed here." Scratching his head as if to shake the bugs off he moaned, "I've got to find a place to get cleaned up and rid of these things."

"C'mon, we'll have to go into Ft. Benton; it's the closest place around. I just left there so I know we can find a bath and get our clothes cleaned."

Del looked at him. "Nope, I was wantin' to avoid that town." Suddenly a fit of scratching took over him; he could feel his skin crawling. He was in misery.

"Okay, okay, I'll go, I guess I don't have much choice right now."

As soon as they got their horses packed up, they rode off together.

"I'm not much looking forward to going back there." Charlie commented after they pulled the horses up to a slow walk just outside of the town. I ran into a bit of trouble, the place is crawling with Canadian mounties."

"What kind a trouble? Del asked. "You don't sound like you're from around here."

"Nope, from far away, across the sea! I've wandered around plenty, but Ireland be my homeland. Left Ireland far behind and took to the seas, traveled the world over. I jumped ship in California. Wanted to see what this great land of America was all about. I worked ranches and mills until I earned enough money to go a little further. And here I am, far from rich, but far from poor. I'm here without papers and the law was about to catch up with me."

"You looking for work too?"

"Ya, I am, but not around here. Need to find a place a little farther away from the border."

They rode on and in town Charlie took them straight to a hotel that offered baths.

They first bought some new clothes and lye soap.

"I needed some new duds anyway." Del commented as he paid for dungarees and a shirt. Their new clothes packaged under their arms they signed in for baths. A young girl showed them the way to the rooms.

"Boil me clothes lassie, and there be a bit extra in the tip. We'll leave the clothes on the floor". Charlie handed the girl some silver.

"As soon as we get cleaned up, I'm going to get some food. I'm getting a bit peckish."

"Well, I could use some food," Del agreed, "but then I have to take care of a little business." Right after breakfast Del found a post office. He had a money order made out for half of the bounty he received for the coyote furs. As he wrote out an envelope to mail it off he wondered if Joe would be surprised to receive it.

They spent the rest of the day and a night staying close to the hotel. The town was busy as wagons, carts and occasional motorcars passed through the streets. Sitting outside the hotel they watched the traffic of people and talked. Suffocating dust surrounded them as the afternoon heat lingered on. Charlie found a newspaper. "Sheep's wool is going for 52 cents a pound. Lots of sheep farmers round these parts. Not much for ranching anymore."

The news was heavy with fighting and death of soldiers in the great war.

"The States are now into the war. There will be more than mounties out looking to round up men for the army now."

Here they were in this quiet mid-western town where time slowly breathed, as town's people went about their business so far removed from the ugliness of broken boys, death and injury. Yet, it wasn't far enough away.

The war had finally dragged the States into the fighting and all available men would be called up to report for duty.

"Del, I can't stay around here. They will be asking questions wantin' to know if I'm registered. Next thing I know, they'll find out I'm here without papers or anything."

Twice they watched a group of mounties pass by. Both of them got a bit nervous and decided they had to move inside.

Over a good supper at the hotel, Del told Charlie his whole story about the homestead and leaving it behind to go back to the States. While he talked, his thoughts turned to the great land up north that he had heard so much about. Charlie was a likeable guy. His Irish accent was intriguing, and he had a direct, honest way of speaking.

Del leaned back in his chair, crossed his arms and studied Charlie's face.

"There's a place we can go, and make some good money, too, if you want to be adventurous. Its tough living in wild country."

Charlie looked at Del with renewed interest. "Adventure is my middle name, what you talking about?"

"Peace River Country. It's far north, up in the Canadian Rockies. I've heard tell of it. It's great trapping country and not much civilization there. A desolate, remote territory where mostly natives and animals live."

Del and Charlie loaded up with as many supplies as they could carry, each with a packhorse, and soon headed out of town going north. They crossed the border back into Canada and steadily worked their way toward Peace River Country. They avoided any big towns and lived off the land. Hunting and fishing along the way, they made camp early in the evenings to rest and let the horses also have a good rest. They traveled several days this way as the summer days beat upon them, hot and sometimes brutal. Finding a river large enough meant a good swim, cooling off and a well needed bath. Finally, they began to leave the prairie behind as the foothills of the mountains began to rise and fall into deep ravines and canyons.

Setting up camp on a riverbank, the two men sat and contemplated a route to best cross deep rushing waters. The early evening light gave them time to set up a rough lean-to for the night. Dark clouds threatened rain and a possible storm. Gathering wood, they piled it to one side and fed the campfire as needed. A large juicy spruce grouse cooked over the flames.

"Have any idea where abouts we are?"

"Em, I would think we are about half way up this mountain, whichever one it may be." Charlie replied as he stoked up the fire a little being careful not to burn the cooking bird.

"Ya know mate", Charlie continued, "I've seen a lot of places, even been to China once, but I have never seen anything as grand as this land. I'm sure happy that I listened to your idea of coming out here."

They had been following a trail for sometime, but hadn't seen a person to talk to in several days. They had found a small lake back down the trail a ways with a few homes, farms and an old fort close by. At the fort, there were several people, many of them natives. They were given direction to follow this trail to travel north toward the next remote trading post.

They had entered Peace River Country of British Columbia, and a beautiful country it was. Tall, tall mountains filled the background under clear deep blue skies. The hills and terrain of the lowlands bloomed with lush trees, tall pines and the greenest of grasses. Rocks were not mere rocks, but large boulders leaning against boulders, forming ledges and ridges along rushing streams of clear pure waters. Waters filled with rainbow trout and mountain white fish. It was here the deer and moose fed and drank along isolated bays. The bald eagles soared above secluded beaches, then pushed high into the skies to perch among the cliffs and large branches reaching over the mountainsides.

As they rode deep into this new territory, they put civilization farther and farther behind; crowded towns with all the luxuries, the world, the war. Here they had only their horses, wildlife and each other for company. Here there was peace, contentment and deep satisfaction living among nature.

Del poured another cup of strong coffee into his tin mug while watching the bird cook, feeling grateful that they were able to catch such a large grouse for their supper. Looking out over the swift water, he mulled over what their best route should be. The ancient trail definitely came to this spot. The river must be higher than usual. After the meal they wandered down stream and around a bend they found where the river narrowed with calm waters at a shallow bay. This would be the place to cross. There was no sense in going further tonight. They had set up camp and had a good place; early morning would be soon enough.

It rained during the night. Morning was warm and still, the ground was wet and raindrops dripped off from the leaves of the trees. Several birds called out and flittered about the brush as Del began to wake up. He pushed back the blanket, which kept him warm during the cool rainy night. The lean-to was just enough shelter so that they were dry and comfortable. A mist spread out over the land covering the mountaintops and hung low over the nearby river. Charlie was up and singing one of his Irish songs as he built up the campfire to make coffee and cook breakfast.

They were just cleaning up the campsite and packing the horses when they heard sounds of something or someone coming through the forest. They both stopped and listened carefully, looking in the same direction. Suddenly, and to their amazement, two Indians came running up to them. The Indians were not threatening, but ran straight to them without hesitating, as if they knew exactly where to find Del and Charlie. They were young men, anxious and in a hurry. With very broken English, they talked loud and pointed down the trail.

"Come with us, we need help, come with us."

They waved their arms motioning Del and Charlie to follow them. Del and Charlie looked at each other, back to the Indians and back to each other. Charlie shrugged his shoulders and arched his eyebrows with apprehension. Del watched the two young Indian men and decided they must really need help of some kind. Maybe one of their people was hurt or sick.

"Is someone hurt?" He asked talking slow and clear.

One of the natives seemed to speak better English than the other. He quickly shook his head.

"My woman needs help. Baby is coming now. Just me and my brother here, we alone with no medicine woman, no one to help her. You come, all white men know medicine."

Del was taken aback, how could he help deliver a baby? He looked at Charlie and softly asked, "You ever delivered a baby before?"

Charlie didn't directly answer him, while his eyes stayed on the Indians he said, "Del, we better go with them. I don't think it be wise to refuse at this point."

"Okay." Del said, "We'll go with you."

The Indians took off on foot running through the woods. Del and Charlie got on their horses and followed them down the trail along the water that led downstream and past the shallow bay where the river narrowed. Not far from there, back in a small clearing of the forest, they reached the Indians' camp. A crude shelter had been hastily built with a deer hide covering the entrance. Only the two young men and the woman were there. Del surmised that they must have been traveling from one tribe to another when the baby decided to make an entrance into the world.

A campfire had been started inside a circle of stones.

"We need some hot water." Del told Charlie. "I will rig up some stones here on the fire. You fetch a kettle from our supplies."

Charlie poured their drinking water into the kettle and gave it to Del for the fire.

Del nervously fished out a few strips of buckskin he had with him. The only thing he could think of to use for string or thread. Squatting down beside him, Charlie asked if he knew what he was doing.

"No", replied Del, "but I grew up on a farm and I've seen plenty of animals born. My mother had nine kids, and I was around when my little brothers were babies. I know this much, we will need something to tie and cut the cord. Let's hope the good Lord does the rest."

Taking the hot water Del washed the buckskin cord, his knife and then his hands. From within the shelter, a scream cried out followed by soft moaning. Del looked at Charlie, "Here we go!"

Del swallowed hard, with fear and anxiety he entered the shelter with Charlie close behind him. The young Indian woman watched them not seeming to care if they were there or not. Long black hair fell loose about her, covering most of her face. Del tried not to look at her. His attention was on the tiny baby that lay on the harsh blood soaked blanket. The infant had arrived on his own, squirming and moving about. "Thank you, God", Del whispered to himself and let out a long sigh.

"Charlie, did you bring that clean shirt?"

Del looked the baby over, awe struck at such a tiny creature. Quickly he worked on tying the umbilical cord, breathing a sigh of relief after he cut it. Until then Del hadn't realized he was holding his breath. Meanwhile, Charlie pulled out his clean shirt along with a few patches of flannel. Del used a piece of the flannel cloth and very softly began to clean the baby off. Awkwardly, he picked him up and wrapped Charlie's clean shirt about him. While Del worked with the baby, Charlie picked up another piece of flannel. Pushing back the hair from the girl's face, he gently wiped off the sweat and tears. A tired smile rewarded his compassion. Slowly, Del laid the baby in the new mother's waiting arms. For the first time, Del took a good look at her and realized she was not much more than a young girl.

"It's a boy." He murmured.

"Nitsiniiyi taki," she whispered looking at Del and Charlie with her dark eyes, then turned her attention to her baby.

"She says thank you." The woman's husband said. He had just entered and was standing behind them. "I say thank you; you good help."

Del and Charlie nodded their heads and moved out of the way to let the Indian see his son.

"That's okay. We will be leaving now, have to get on our way." Del said as they turned to leave.

Quickly, before the Indians should demand that they stay, they got on their horses, turned toward the trail and back to the shallow bay to cross the river. The morning sun was not yet high in the sky. They could still get in a full day's travel.

# *Chapter 26*
## MARK DEBRAL'S TRADING POST

The old trail followed an Indian path along the shore of the Pine River. Deep into the tall timbers of the Northwest Territory they steadily climbed. The early morning was cool for a midsummer day. Del wrapped his flannel shirt about him, buttoned it up tight and pulled his hat on. There was hardly a breeze in the air. Nothing in the forest stirred. The snorting of the horses and the clomping of their feet along the rough terrain broke the silence. The men started out the day by leading the horses, as the path became hard to follow through dense brush and broken trees.

"Are you sure we haven't lost the trail all together?" Charlie asked as he took off his hat and slapped it about his head chasing away the horseflies. "We can hardly walk through here, there's no way wagons went this way."

Del looked up and turned around searching the area. "Ya, I know it sure looks like it hasn't been used in a long time. We might have strayed off the beaten path aways back before we made camp. Hard to tell just where it went at times, especially near dark. But, I figure if we stay near the river we're bound to come back to it. I see a bog hole up ahead at the foot of a hill. We better get back on the horses to cross it or else find a way around it."

Charlie walked up beside Del to see what he was talking about.

"Doesn't look that bad, let's just ride across it. The horses can make it. I have a feelin' that we'll find something on the other side of that hill."

Del laughed out loud, "Sure, we'll see another hill, most likely."

They had been traveling for days. Del was tired and it didn't seem like they would ever find this trading post they were supposed to be headed for. The fish they ate last night still stayed with him, even after morning coffee. Skipping breakfast, they chewed on hardtack as they walked their way through the brush. He spared cooking breakfast in hopes they would find meat of some kind to prepare for a full meal later in the day. Supplies were drastically low. "Anything but fish," he thought: that was one thing they had found plenty of.

Charlie had been right; they easily rode the horses through the low bog. Arriving on top of the hill, Del pulled Blaze to a stop. Pushing back his hat, he looked around in amazement! In front of them a large open meadow slopped down toward the river. Hobbling the horses where they could feast on the long grass, Del and Charlie walked to the edge of the meadow. They could see for miles out over a valley. They were high above the tree tops which spread out over rolling hills, meeting taller mountains in the distance.

Down near the river, in the shelter of some pines, was a large cabin with two barns and a corral holding several horses.

"Yee haa! Charlie yelled, "We found it! The trading post!"

Mounting the horses they rode down to the ranch. A man walked out of the barn to greet them. At the same time, a woman and three children came out onto the open porch. Soon, two older children followed. Del instinctively knew this was not the trading post.

"How do ya do?" Del asked as he pushed his hat back and sat back further in his saddle. "I'm Del and this is my partner, Charlie. We are looking for Mark Debral's Trading Post."

"Yup," Charlie joined in. "We was hoping this was it."

The man looked at them and his eyes took in the packhorses loaded down with gear and animal hides. "Sorry to disappoint ya. I'm David Brant; this is my wife, Millie, and our children. We settled here two years ago, but you're on the right path. The trading post is just down river a few more miles. This here is the East Pine." He made a sweeping motion with his arm, taking in the river that ran by his farm. "You follow this till it meets up with the West Pine and that's where you will find Debral's Trading post."

Del was relieved. Not only were they going in the right direction, but they were almost there.

David looked at his wife and said, "I'm sure Millie has the coffee on and there is plenty of stew left from the mule deer I took in the other day. Come in and eat, we'd love to hear some news. Don't see many people to talk to."

Millie assured them that there was plenty and, as anxious as Del and Charlie were to reach their destination, they were hungry.

The Brant's were eager to talk. They usually made a trip to the trading post about every two or three weeks. Sometimes the whole family would go and they would stop and visit other settlers along the way and many times meet up with families there at the post. The mail would come in about once a week or so during the warm months and they would get whatever provisions they needed.

"Do you trap?" Del asked David.

"Uh huh, trapping and hunting through the winter keeps us alive. I have a trap line I work, just a small one, but big enough for just one fellow to take care of."

"That's what Charlie and I plan on doing. We're going to make a place up here somewhere and do some major trapping."

"Yup," David said nodding his head. "You can do alright with a trapping business. That's if you're tough enough. Its wild up here and the winters are mighty tough. I've heard tell of some trap lines for sale up north. If you ask Mark Debral he might know of something."

Del and Charlie shared a look at each other; a look that clearly showed unspoken gratification.

"We'll be sure to do that," Del said as he was getting up out of his chair. "That's just what we're looking for."

By the time they finished the well-needed meal, the day had warmed considerably. Del and Charlie gave thanks to their unexpected hosts and were soon on their way.           Following the river they came upon the lost trail and keenly began to search for the merging of the East and West Pine.

# Chapter 27
## THE TRADING POST

The trail was easy to follow now and it was late the same day they came to the trading post. The waters of the Pine ran much deeper and swifter here.

Tying the horses to a railing out front, they walked past a group of Indians. The Indians had set up camp near the large cabin that served as the trading post. The men, women and children gathered around and watched them with curiosity. None of them spoke.

The big front door was wide-open letting in the summer breeze and much needed light. The large room was filled and overflowing. Baskets and boxes of goods covered the floor. The walls held large shelves containing tools and hand made Indian crafts; snow shoes, baskets and pottery, along with blankets of all sizes and colors.

"Hello, hello, hello!" boomed a loud voice. A large man came out from behind some boxes to greet them.

"I don't think I've seen you around here before", he said as he shook hands first with Del, then with Charlie. "Mark Debral is the name, this is my place. Sorry fer the mess. We just got back with a load of supplies, three wagonloads of stuff here. We're just trying to get it sorted out and put away."

"We're headin' north, wantin' to set up some trap lines."

As soon as the words were out of Charlie's mouth, Mark looked at him. "You must be Irish! Some folks settled in down south of here and they all talk the same way. They came all the way over from Ireland."

Charlie nodded his head but didn't answer. He started looking around the room and soon got busy seeing what was there.

"You sure have a lot of stock, you must get good trade." Del filled in for Charlie's lack of response.

"I have to bring all this in by wagon, usually get a couple of men and take three wagons down to meet up with the boat in the Peace River. Takes a good trip. More and more folks beginnin' to settle in here and take up homesteads, so more is needed. You fellas lookin' to settle here?"

"Not a homestead," Del said, shaking his head and sliding his hands in his pockets. He continued to talk, immediately taking a liking to Mark Debral.

"We want to do some trapping here in these parts, hoping to set up a trap line. We stopped at Dave Brant's place along the way. He told us you might know of something for sale."

Mark contemplated that for a moment, rubbing his hand over his fuzzy beard.

"There's not as many trappers out here as there use to be. But, no, I haven't heard of any for sale. People come and go here a lot. If you stick around awhile you might hear of something."

Del's disappointment showed on his face. With an unconscious sigh he turned to look for Charlie.

"Well, we're in need of grub and supplies and we got some hides that we've taken along our trip."

"You can make yourself to home here. There's places right around here you can make camp until you decide which way you're goin'." Mark replied. "Let's get those furs in here, see what ya got."

Del and Charlie set up camp in the shelter of some big oaks not far from the post and on the other side of where the Indians had temporarily settled.

Indian children ran around and often would run past them laughing and chasing each other. It didn't take long after they were settled for the Indians to invite them into their camp. They sat on tree stumps and broken logs, talked and told stories, legends passed down from the old ones. Many included stories of bears, very large grizzly bears. The women brought food out and shared it with all of them. Del enjoyed the Indian families and with interest, watched how the women took care of their young. While the men talked, a small baby cried and fussed. The baby's mother took him out of the cradleboard, gently washed his bare bottom and took him inside their tent. Del assumed she was feeding him. Shortly, she came back outside and laid the baby on a blanket. He stretched, kicked and looked around, completely free of diapers or swaddling clothes. The mother took the board and totally cleaned out the inside. She then placed fresh clean moss inside. Picking up the baby, she wrapped him in a light cotton blanket before putting him back in his moss filled cradleboard. Clean, dry and happy, the baby was content and soon fell back to sleep.

A few days later, Del was tending to the horses as Charlie cooked some breakfast. A dense fog was beginning to lift as the air warmed with the early sunrise. Two wagons, each pulled by a team of horses, rolled down the trail toward the little colony consisting of campers and the trading post.

Before the first wagon had fully come to a stop, three lively children jumped out from under the canvas cover. A man held the horses quiet while a woman made her way down from the seat. She smoothed a strand of blonde hair back from her face while she watched the Indian children that had gathered around them. The Indian children soon fled back to their encampment, their curiosity satisfied. A boy sat in the front seat of the second wagon driven by a young man. The travelers looked about, taking in the scene of the river and the few campers strewn about. The woman called to her children and they all went inside the trading post. The two men walked toward the riverbank and seemed to be in deep conversation while they looked out across the area up to the mountain peaks. They turned toward the wagons, both shaking their heads. Stopping at the well, one fellow pulled up the wooden well bucket and began to lavishly drink from the dipper. When finished, he handed it over to his friend. Del and Charlie sauntered over and introduced themselves. They soon learned that the two men where brothers, Paul and Melvin Jackson; the woman and the four children where Paul's family. Traveling from Missouri to the Northwest Territory, they planned to settle on a homestead. Now, finally, after two years of roaming, the only thing between them and the new land that they searched for was the big Pine River and one last mountain to cross.

Later that day, Mark Debral walked out to the campsite looking for Del and Charlie. They had just gotten back to camp after doing some hunting for supper. Mark, pulled out a pouch of tobacco and before taking some, offered it to both of them. Charlie took a pinch but Del shook his head. Mark stood with his arms crossed. "Ya know fellas, I'm more than a little worried about this family here. They're fixin' to cross this river and it ain't going to be easy. The river has been running high and mighty strong. These guys aren't no mountain men; they're just plum ole plowboys. Why they'll most likely lose everything they got and drown all those children, too." Mark spit into the long grass and shook his head, "I hate to see them try it. But, I was thinking, you fellas just might help them out, if you would."

He said it almost as a question but more as a matter of fact looking first to Del and then to Charlie. Real concern showed clearly on his large face. "I'd even throw in some free meals for ya for however long it takes to get them across that river," he added.

Charlie looked at Del. "What ya say? Wanna give it a bloody try?"

"Well, sure," Del said slowly, "I guess we could sure give them a hand." Mark was happy with that and before he left to go back to the cabin, he told them to let him know if they needed anything from the store that would help them out.

Alone, Del quietly walked to the waters' edge and looked out over the river and across to the other side. It sure was going to be some doing to get those wagons and horses across that water. His thoughts turned to the family. Paul and his wife were about his age. He had watched them with envy. They had a dream and they both lived and worked together for this land beyond the mountain. They shared and cared for each other. As Del watched them, he sensed what he was missing out of his life. If things had been different; but they weren't. It was what it was. He turned back toward the camp thinking they had lots of work to do and he better get some plans made up.

# Chapter 28

## CURLY AND COWBOY

It took a few days for the men to get the family across the river. Because of the lack of lumber on hand, they took apart the Jackson's wagons to build a scow. This worked out nicely. The following day they were ready. Stella Jackson didn't want to be on the initial trip across; she wanted to make sure it would work first. So the first cargo to cross was the furniture. Once the makeshift scow made it safely across and back, then the children and Mrs. Jackson took their turn. They sat down on the boards, hanging on to each other. Slowly the men guided the scow across the rough waters, using long poles to maneuver. The older boys bravely watched over the family's personal possessions while the younger ones hung on to their mother, hiding their faces against her body. The water splashed and rose up over the boards onto wooden boxes and baskets. Due to the strong arms of the four men, along with Del and Charlie's guidance, they reached the other side. Del jumped off and held the scow steady until the others were able to help him pull it up enough on shore to stay put and not wash away. Leaving the family and possessions safely on the other side, they went back to pick up another load. It took many crossings to get it all. There were farm tools, blacksmith tools, a plow and most everything you could think of. The cattle and horses came last.

Finally with everything and everyone safely across, the men began the task of putting the wagons back together. There, they spent the night, on the opposite side of the river. Sitting around a large campfire, they enjoyed a meal that Mark had sent along for them. They drank coffee and talked. The Jacksons were very grateful for the help. They were very excited about reaching their new land and talked about it continuously. After traveling for so long, now they only had one more mountain to cross. The mountain had no trail and it was too steep to make a road for the wagons. They would have to break a new road gradually working around the mountain. This meant cutting trees, brush, and going around rocks, ravines and swamps. It would be very rough going. Although it was the end of their long journey, it may very well be the roughest with nothing to follow into this wilderness.

The younger children became tired. Del watched as Stella talked to them and cuddled the youngest in her arms. Paul took the child and helped her stand up. She was about to set out bedding and blankets for the youngsters and settle them in for the night. She turned to Del and Charlie and said, "Thank you so much. We are so grateful." Her face was waned with weary but her eyes were bright and sparkling blue.

Again, Del thought of Roxie; it must be the depth of those eyes that triggered a memory. "Glad we could help you out," he said as he nodded his head in acknowledgement of her thanks. "Have a good night," he murmured.

While Stella took care of the children Paul and Charlie talked while they took a short walk around the wagons. Charlie gave advice to Paul on how to clear a trail for their route over the mountain.

In the early morning Paul and Melvin shook hands with Del and Charlie and said their goodbyes. Del and Charlie had towed along with them Mark's small rowboat to use for returning. Sliding the boat back into the river they climbed in and rowed back toward the trading post.


Getting back to their campsite they went to look up Mark and tell him the family was safely across the river. Mark had been watching for them and was eager to introduce them to a couple of fellows that had arrived the day before.

"Del, Charlie, I knew you could get them across, if anyone could do it you could. Look, look here, I want you to meet a couple fellows. They are out to find a trap line too, just like you." Two burly woodsmen stood beside Mark. Although they were still young men, Del judged them to be a little older and tougher. One guy put out his hand to Del and then to Charlie and said, "Howdy, I'm Curly and this is my partner, Cowboy." Cowboy just nodded his head as Curly did all of the talking.

"Mark had told us about you fellas looking for a trap line. Maybe it's something we could get together on. We know of a trap line for sale but they're asking more money than what we could come up with. Maybe it's something you would consider going in on with us to share."

Del and Charlie invited Curly and Cowboy out to their camp. They stirred up some vittles and coffee and got to know each other well enough to find out what kind of characters these guys were. Seemed like they were much like themselves: hunters, trappers, loggers, men of the mountain. They lived the way they wanted for no other reason, with no set direction or greater purpose than to find some wildlife and make good money off the furs. No one asked where anyone came from or why they were there, no need for that.

"Just where is this trap line anyway?" Del asked. Curly stirred a map in the dirt with a stick. Making a large circle, he pointed to the top. "This is all Peace River country, and we are here on the River Pine, where the two rivers join, the East and The West Pine." He drew a straight line through the center. "The trap line is north and east of the Pine; a large trap line with four cabins already on it."

Del pondered the dirt map thinking he just might have struck gold. This is what he was looking for, right here in Peace River Country, east of the Pine.

"The trap line is for sale for a good sum of $400. This includes the four trappers' cabins and 400 traps. We could only come up with $100 between us," Curly explained.

Del looked at Charlie quizzically not knowing for sure how much money Charlie carried with him, or how much he would be willing to put up. Charlie turned toward their camp and motioned to Del to follow. Rubbing his face and then the back of his head he spoke quietly. "I could match what they have Del, what ya think?"

"Yaaa," Del breathed a long sigh. "That leaves $200. I would like to see what it is. If we have to, maybe we could work out a deal of some kind. Even with four of us sharing, it sounds big enough to be worth looking into." They turned back to the other two men.

Del spoke. "We'd like to see this trap line and talk to the owner about it. Maybe we can do business." The four men shook hands and the twosome became a foursome.

# Chapter 29
## THE TRAP LINE

They traveled deeper into Peace River country. The land gave way from mountainous terrain to rolling soft green-forested hills. Together the four of them traveled the path that Curly and Cowboy had recently crossed.

Ed Finney's trading post was a busy place. A big steam powered stern-wheeler was waiting in the water just off the shore. Indian people worked many of the several tasks. Two barns, a warehouse, a blacksmith shop and several cabins surrounded the large log combination store and trading post. A few women were tending to large gardens among the buildings.

Although the railroad was quickly spreading across the country, it hadn't found its way to this part of the world yet. Travel was by wagon or boat and sometimes dog sled in the winter. Inside the trading post, Curley and Cowboy looked for Ed Finney, the owner. A man working behind the counter told them that he was up the hill at his house putting shingles on a new addition. Del was curious about the paddleboat and asked where it was going.

"It carries mail, passengers and freight going to and from Peace River."

"Peace River!" Del exclaimed with surprise. "We're that close to Peace River?"

"The boats follow a channel into a river that flows to the Peace. Within the last seven or eight years the government opened up land for settlement. Many travelers have started passing through here spending the night and eating meals.

Got a menu over here if you're interested."

He handed the menu to Del, so Del read it out loud:

"Moose steak dinner – 35 cents

Corn meal mush – 25 cents

Calves liver & bacon 25 cents

Stuffed chicken dinner – 50 cents
Beef pot pie and egg dumplings - 25 cents
Pie - 10 cents".

"Well, if Ed Finney ain't going nowhere, I think we better have a bite to eat. This here menu looks really good. I'd like that beef pot-pie and egg dumplings and a piece of raspberry pie." With that Del pulled some change out of his pocket and counted out 35 cents.

They ate heartily sitting at a long, roughly hewed table. Before they were finished, a big burly man walked over, pulled up a chair and sat down with them.

"Ed Finney here. I was told you fellows is looking fer me?" He sat with his arms crossed on the table and didn't offer to shake hands. Then he noticed Curly and Cowboy. A surprised expression crossed his face.

"Ah, you guys were here not too long ago, I remember you. You was askin about that trap line. Change yer mind?"

Curley spoke up. "Ya see, we found a couple other guys that are interested." Pointing his fork at Del and Charlie, he went on. "They's looking for a trap line, too, and we thought maybe the four of us might go in together on it if we can make you a deal."

"Huh, $400, that's it, can't take any less. It belongs to two brothers. They've given me permission to sell it for them. There's a trail runs northeast into Wabi Valley over to Graveyard Creek. Has a main cabin and four good trappers' cabins. And it comes with 400 traps."

"We would like to see it," Del spoke up. "Sounds like a good investment to me, but I want to look at what we're buying into. I've never bought a pig-in-a-poke yet!"

Ed squinted, taking a serious look at Del. "Okay!" His big hand slapped the table. "First thing in the morning we can start out. It'll take a few days to cover the whole thing. You fellas want a room for the night?"

They traveled northeast the next day, all riding horseback. They covered good ground and in the afternoon they came to the creek and the main cabin. It was a large well-built cabin with a veranda across the front. It hadn't been used in awhile and was boarded up tight. They pulled off boards covering the windows to let in light, opened the door and aired the place out. There was lots of evidence of mice and squirrels that had nested in the large shelter. Checking out the fireplace, it seemed clean enough to be used again. Other than that, they only fixed up the place enough to make it comfortable for the night, setting out blankets on the bunks. The heat of the late summer day brought out the bugs and mosquitoes that swarmed about them. They were bad enough going along the trail, but here by the creek they were much worse. The men gathered together some sticks and dry grass and built a smudge. It

113

helped somewhat to get rid of the bugs as they worked about. They scouted out the creek and explored the land for a short distance. They went back to the main cabin that night, cooked up some food and sat around the table playing cards until dark.

The next morning they followed the trail to the first trappers' cabin on the line. It was a small log building with two small windows. Inside it held a rough hewn wooden table cut from logs, log chairs, and a double bunk, one over the other. A small stone fireplace was the only source of heat, cozy enough to spend a winter night. Here there was long green grass, an open creek running strong, shrubs and trees in full blossom. It was difficult to picture a winter scene.

They took a few days to finish touring the rest of the trap line, but Del had made up his mind the very first day that this was going to be his trap line. His and Charlie's, Curly's and Cowboy's; partners. He would have the most invested but if that's what it took, then that would be okay. This was what he wanted!

Back at the trading post they signed the papers and purchased the trap line. They bought supplies, food and traps along with grain for the horses. They took the rest of the summer to clean up all of the cabins, stock them and have them ready before beginning to set traps. Each small trapper's cabin had to have a supply of wood, cooking utensils, snow shovel, a lantern with kerosene and a fresh mattress made of canvas and stuffed with grass. Fall in this country came early and it would soon be arriving.

# Chapter 30
## WORKING THE TRAP LINE

The four little cabins were cleaned, repaired and stocked as summer neared the end. The days were getting shorter and cooler, but fall weather wasn't yet in sight. The supplies were low and the men had decided to make a trip back to Finney's to stock up while they could.

Del flopped the last of the flapjacks onto a plate and moved the pan off the woodstove. Charlie grabbed up the tin coffee pot and poured it out into the mugs as Curley and Cowboy took a seat at the table. It was barely daybreak as rays of light began to slip through the small windows of the cabin.

"Ya know fellas," Del began in between mouthfuls of food, "I've been giving it some thought and I think we have a long trek to make between our four cabins. We have time before the trapping season begins. We could easily put up another cabin or two."

The three looked at him and then went back to their food. "You ever build a cabin before?" Curly asked.

"Ya, sure have. I've built cabins, houses and barns. Done plenty of building," Del replied. "Won't take us long with the four of us working on it. We are heading to Finney's today; we can pick up what we need for materials to build them and supplies to stock them."

"And just where would we put these cabins?" Curley asked.

"Well, I been thinking on it and I reckon we could use one between here and the first cabin. It would be a couple miles out, back where the creek bends off to the west."

"Why not?" Cowboy put in, "What else we got to do?"

Soon after they returned from their trip to the trading post they began work on a new cabin. The men worked from sunup to sundown cutting trees and laying logs. The new cabin took shape quickly. It was much like the others, a single room with a low roof. It went so well they decided to build another off in the opposite direction from the main cabin.

Working on the last cabin Charlie and Del finished the chimney using ashes and water mixed together to adhere the small field stones together. Cowboy and Curly were building a bunk, the last of the furnishings.

"There's the last of it," Del said as he patted the last stone into place. Sitting on the roof, he turned and looked about him. "We're just in time, Charlie. Now we can set to work on our traps."

The leaves were turning colors as the trees on the mountains beamed a brilliant red and yellow among the tall evergreens. Darkness came early and a cold frost had already hit the region. Del was eager to begin working the trap line.

Now with six cabins, when the snow got too deep for the horse and pack horse to travel the line, the distance would be much better for them to hike on snowshoes while pulling a sled full of furs.

Things went well for Del and his trapping companions on the trap line. They all went out in different directions to set up the traps, each spending the night in a different cabin. After a few days they would meet back at the main cabin bringing what furs they had caught. They worked hard and worked together. Sometimes it was days before they saw each other. There were times one would go ahead and set traps and one would come behind the next day checking them and picking up the catch. The trap would then have to be reset. Other times they would each go in a different direction, staying the night in the first cabin they came to. Then, in the morning, they would go back to check the traps they had set the day before.

The traps had to have care, too. A chain was used to fasten the trap to a stake so the animal couldn't drag it away. Sometimes a chain or the pan that springs the trap would break. There was always plenty to do. After a few weeks of avid trapping and when supplies got low, they would take turns going to the trading post. Charlie and Del usually went together.

Del had been out on the trap line for a few days. He was not far from one of the cabins and it was late afternoon. His packhorse was heavy with furs; a good catch. He had skinned out each animal so as not to have so much weight to carry, but when he got to the cabin he still had to flesh out each one. A few inches of snow had fallen during the day covering the ground and clinging to the trees. He would not be able to use the horses much longer if it kept accumulating. The little cabin was a welcome sight. He was tired and the cold wind was beginning to seep through his clothes. Opening the door, he went straight to the fireplace to start a fire and get the place warmed up. With relief, he saw that the last one there had laid out starter sticks and it was ready and waiting for him, all he had to do was strike a match and start the fire. He then took care of the horses, unloaded the skins and set to work fleshing out each one. The beaver was especially quite a job to flesh out; all the fat and tissue had to be scraped off.

It was dark by the time he finished his last skin. Inside, a lantern that hung from a beam overhead cast plenty of light when he lit it. The smithy at the post had made iron grates to use on the fireplace. Placing a pan on the grate, he cooked his supper and hungrily ate while sitting at the small handmade table. There was enough fresh snow to melt and heat, but he knew it would be best to save the precious drinking water as much as he could. After cleaning up his tin plate and cooking pan, he went outside to check on the horses one more time. Clouds covered the stars and moon making a very dark night. Blaze nickered looking for a treat as he came near. "There boy, it's alright," Del murmured as he slipped a small carrot out of his pocket. "Tomorrow will be a shorter day and we will head back to the main cabin and your barn." The horses didn't have much shelter here, even though Del had hobbled them under some full pines out of the wind. Giving the packhorse the last little carrot, he gave them a pat and left them for the night. Back inside he stoked up the fire. The crackle and sizzling of the burning wood blended with the night wind whispering around the pines, blocking out his own silence. He curled up on the bunk and was soon sound asleep.

Del was up early, put on a pot of coffee and ate his breakfast before the sun was fully up. He let the fire die out while he made up the bunk and cleaned the coffee pot and pans from breakfast. The last thing he did was to clear out the ashes and whittle out shavings from the wood, piling them up for starter sticks, leaving the fire pre-built and ready for the next trapper.

# Chapter 31
## THE BEAVER

Traveling the trapline alone Del would often get restless and give in to the urge to wander. There was always more of the countryside to explore, wanting to know what was on the other side of a hill or just around one more bend. He learned the countryside well and eventually wandered farther and farther away being gone from the camp for longer periods of time. Never without his trusty compass, he always found his way back.

Charlie, Curley and Cowboy became use to his ventures and didn't worry if he didn't show up back at the main cabin for a few days. Del was not one to say to anyone what he was doing. Often he didn't know himself how long he would be gone. It might be a week or so before any of the fellow trappers saw him, not knowing if he was out on the line or just exploring and then he would just show up.

It was during one of these excursions that Del discovered a lake. Moving off toward a clearing Del thought he saw glimpses of water between the trees and brush off in the distance. The snow wasn't deep and carefully Blaze made a path through the woods coming out to the shores of a small lake. A hawk glided overhead across a blue sky, a sunny day, warm enough to travel comfortable without layers of clothes. Patches of ice near the water's edge sparkled in the bright sunlight. The water was open and moving slightly making Del believe that a river or creek emptied into this lake. There were dead trees among tall pines along the shore and small islands scattered across. He tethered Blaze where he could munch on some brush. Walking closer to the shore he noticed something swimming in the water. It was out far enough that he couldn't make out what it was for sure, but it was big and moving right along. He decided it had to be a beaver. Quickly he went back to where he had left Blaze and got his rifle. Taking careful aim he shot and the animal stopped moving and lay floating in the water. He had hit it, but now the problem was how to get it. It was too far out in the water to get to. He couldn't let it go, he had killed it now he had to retrieve it somehow. Turning back toward the woods he went looking for some deadwood. He found enough dead logs small enough and dry enough to use. Using his hatchet he chopped them down to size. Tying a rope around each end he had a small raft. He worked quickly and deftly dragging the raft to the lake he looked out for his kill. Sure enough the animal was still floating in the water. A long stick that he found on the shore worked just right for a pole and he carefully pushed himself off into the lake. Water seeped up over the edge of his makeshift raft but luckily his boots kept him dry. He was right, it was a beaver, a very large heavy beaver as he pulled it out of the water and onto the raft. Good thing he hadn't let this one go it was a perfect fur, well worth the effort to retrieve it. This guy was at least a good seventyfive pounds. Once back on shore he immediately skinned out the beaver. To Del's surprise it was full of unborn kits. He had never seen unborn kits before. They were tiny, about the size of one of his fingers and covered with dark skin

He decided to make camp there and spend the night rather than hike back to the cabin. There was enough daylight left to rig up a lean-too for shelter out of brush twigs and a canvass that he always carried. Then he built a camp fire close enough to keep warm. With that finished he went hunting for his supper. He followed rabbit tracks until he came to a den. Snowshoe rabbits scattered everywhere running in circles. He only needed one good one, a big gray hare would do. He skinned out the animal and added the hide to his catch. He hadn't brought the packhorse but Blaze could easily carry what he had.

Fixing up a spit he cooked the rabbit over the open fire. He would have enjoyed some coffee but water out of his canteen would have to do. Laying a second canvass on the ground he rolled out his blankets and used his saddle for a pillow. The stars were bright and a big moon lit up the night. Del lay awake for a long time listening to the howling of coyotes and wolves; animals of the wild, roaming their terrain throughout the night. He knew he was trespassing on their territory. After awhile he would doze and wake often, adding wood to his fire.

When morning arrived Del had no desire to go back to the cabin. Instead he and Blaze left the lake and road east going even further away. He found the creek that ran into the lake and followed it for sometime. Eventually the creek lead to a large river. A well worn trail followed the rivers edge. People had used this trail recently Del thought. Indians probably or settlers, it had to lead to somewhere. He had only ridden about a few miles when a familiar sight came into view. He had arrived at Mark Debral's trading post. The River he had been following for the last few miles was the East Pine.

Mark was alone in the store and he was readily surprised when Del walked through the door.

"Looky here! You found your way back! How ya been and where ya goin?"

Del shook hands with Mark, happy to see him. "I sure would like some of that coffee if ya got any ready."

"Come and sit by the stove, I've got plenty of coffee."

So they sat and talked. Del told Mark all about the trapline and how the partnership was working out. Soon the best part of the day was gone.

"Lets take care of your horse, Mark offered. Put him in the barn and we'll get some grub going. You ain't goin nowhere tonight."

"Yup, okay," Del replied. "I got a few skins out there too. The best beaver hide you ever did see."

Fetching the skins he told Mark his story about shooting the beaver and then having to fetch him out of the lake.

"This is a grand skin!" Mark explained "I can give you a pretty penny for it. You were very lucky you know. If she hadn't been full of them kits she would have sunk to the bottom as soon as you shot her."

Mark fixed them up some supper and they talked and told stories well into the night. The two men became good friends. With lack of sleep the night before and the late night talk, Del slept into the morning. When he awoke the sun was bright in the sky and he could hear Mark working about in the store. He had found a route from the trap line cabin to Mark Debral's and it wasn't all that far to travel. He would come here more often.

"I'm sure you'll be heading back home today." Mark said as he poured Del a mug of coffee. "I packed some food fer your trip."

Mark had meant the cabin at the trap line when he said going home. But as soon as he heard the word home, Del thought of his ma and pa and the kids back home in New York. He had been thinking about them off and on lately, it had been a long time since he had sent word home. They had no idea where he was and they had no way of writing to him.

Del gave this some thought as he drank his coffee and ate the fried eggs and potatoes that Mark had cooked for him.

"Before I leave I want to buy a writing pad of paper and a pen too. I'd like to write to my family back home. Can I tell them I can pick up mail here if they write to me?"

Mark looked at him with concern. "Certainly, certainly" he said in his booming voice. "Your folks need to hear from you. They must be plum crazy with worry, not knowing where you are or whats happened to ya!" He quickly went to the shelf and found writing paper and a pen. "The mail will be going out the day after tomorrow."

# Chapter 32

## A Winter on the Trap line

In October the weather moved toward winter. A heavy snowstorm hit one day but the following day a breeze blew across the land as warm as summer and the ground was bare again. The trapping continued bringing in many hides including beaver, mink, marten, and fox. Occasionally the men would set out hunting with the rifles and shoot a caribou or sometimes a moose. The dried meat would last for a long time.

It wasn't until late in November when the real cold hit hard, freezing over the creeks and lakes. There were spells of squalls and bitter cold and then days they would wake up to mild clear weather with frosty nights. They would spend their time during these days cutting wood and hauling it to the cabins. They built a good sized sled and hooked it up to the horses to draw the wood. Often the wind would blow enough of the snow away and make it possible for the horses to draw the sled on the frozen water. During this time the traps and snares began coming up empty and it was rare to come in with a good catch.

The cabin door burst open and an icy cold gust of wind blew about the room as Curly tromped in. Slamming the door he stomped his feet loosening the caked on ice and snow. As he removed his heavy wool coat and hat he grumbled and growled a low guttural sound from his throat. Cowboy had just finished changing into warm clothes and was hanging his wet pants on a peg on the wall, near enough to the wood stove to dry them out. Charlie was busy cooking a rabbit and preparing what he called his Irish stew. Del sat in the corner of the room sewing up holes in his favorite pair of socks. All eyes flew to Curly as the men tried to understand what he was saying.

"You all right?" Cowboy asked after Curly proceeded to throw his wet clothes around, all the while still grumbling loudly.

Cowboy was a quiet man, moved slow and easygoing, the opposite of his large partner. Curly was excitable, loud and boystras but generally good natured.

"No" he shouted. I'm far from all right! I'm tired of this place, this cold god- forsaken land." He sat down in a chair to remove his boots. "I trekked from here to kingdom come and back again. I end up with two lousy martens in the traps. I almost had a good-looking mink but it got away from me before I could get a shot at it. Its gotta be 20 below out there." He moaned and rubbed his cold feet.

Charlie turned back to his cooking. "I think we're all a little tired of this place and the cold and winter. A trip back to Finnie's post might do us some good, and we can get a decent meal, something other than my great Irish stew. Besides, he added, we are low on a few things and we could stock up on supplies."

Del finished his socks and put them away in a cedar wood box near his bunk. "I could go for that, I sure would like to taste a decent meal, anything but Irish stew! Maybe even have some kind of pie."

It was during a mild spell in January that the four of them set off together to visit the trading post. They were all looking forward to getting that good meal but also eager for any news that Ed Finnie had heard of.

The place was busy when they got there. Other trappers from different parts had the same idea and had taken advantage of the good weather to pick up supplies. Together they carried in a load of furs and set them out for Ed Finnie to take care of. Then they looked around and picked out things they needed. Charlie had a list, coffee, tea, flour, salt and ammunition. It didn't take them long. The next thing they headed for was to see what was being offered for dinner.

Other men sat around the table too busy eating to talk much. Del, Charlie, Curly and Cowboy each finished up their meal with a good sized piece of apple pie made from last fall's dried apples. Pushing themselves away from the table they took their cups filled with hot coffee and moved over to sit on wooden chairs scattered around the wood stove.

They joined a few trappers already sitting around the wood stove. One was an older fellow with snow-white hair and beard. He removed a corncob pipe from his mouth to talk. "Nice bunch of furs you fellows brought in. Where's your place?"

Del was the first to answer. "We got a trap line not far from here."

"Ya? You all in it together?" As the old man smoked he kept one hand on his pipe and the other hand gripping his large suspenders, which crossed a wool plaid shirt that had seen many days wear.

"The four of us", Curly said, "we just bought it up last year."

The old man nodded his head and looked at them with interest. "Newcomers! How far north in the territory have ya been?"

"This is it," Curly told him. "I've been no further, unless these fella's have before I knew um."

Del and Charlie shook their heads, sitting back, their stomachs heavy, the warm stove making them drowsy. They didn't feel much like talking at the moment, but as the old fellow began talking they perked up and listened to his story. As the men listened the old timer had many stories of the old days and how it use to be.

"I been west through those mountains and I been north clear to the Yukon and back. There is nothing like the Peace River country. You'll never see anything like it." The old man paused, puffed on his pipe and looked thoughtfully at each of them before he went on.

"The way this country is now is pretty much how it looked in the beginning. I first arrived at the Peace River area during the days of the big gold rush back in the 1870's. I was young, just about twenty years old, and by the time I arrived to pan for gold the rich vanes were gone. The frenzy for gold had tapered off.

"Gold rush? Here, they found gold here?" Charlie and Del looked at each other quizzically. Charlie sat up to the edge of his chair wanting to know more. "We never heard of gold being found here before."

The old fellow chuckled and as he did so, his round belly shook. "Oh yes, gold was washed down the Peace River from Finlay's branch, one of its sources, and it made thousands of sane men plumb crazy with gold fever. Towns sprung up out of nowhere as men poured in from all over. Timber and logs were chopped out to make new trails. Soon there were more men than provisions could take care of. Robberies of flour, bacon and whatever could be taken began to spread widely. It would take months for any mail to come through. That was all more than forty years ago now."

The old man had all of their attention. He crossed his arms over his belly and went on.

"My journey took me to the bottom of the valley near the rushing creek of Germansen. There I lived among the miners. Let me tell you, the miner is a queer sort of fellow. The miner has ever got his dream. His golden paradise is always away up in some half unreachable spot in a wilderness of mountains. Nature locked her treasurers of gold and silver in deep mountain caverns not to be found easily."

"A miner's life is different. He can't settle down, at least not for a long time. He's obsessed with a strange fascination and cannot give up the wild, free life. I seen men lose more money in one night at poker than would have kept him decently for five years. They easily put two dollars into the ground to dig one dollar out of it."

"I probably would have left when most of the others did, but I had gotten to know this young Indian girl. Prettiest thing you ever did see." The old man's face lit up with the memory. "I married her when the chaplain made his rounds to these parts. I took up trapping and settled on the flats by the river, a piece large enough for a nice garden. We survived well and raised a little family." He smiled more to himself than to anyone else, looked up at his audience and went on.

"Hudson Bay was the major trading post of the era and they covered most of the whole Northwest Territory. After the gold rush many independent traders such as Ed Finnie moved in taking away some of the trade. There are still many Hudson Bay posts in the area. They'd give a good price for those furs you brought in."

"Tell us", Charlie said in his rich Irish accent, "Just how does a man find this Hudson Bay post from here?"

"Ahhh, don't tell big Ed that I told ya, but you go three or four days travel to the big Peace River. Once you hit the Peace, head west and you will come to a place they now call Hudson's Hope."

The four men spent the night and the next day left the post to go back to their trapping cabin. As Del and Charlie went out to bring in their horses they talked about the Hudson Bay post.

"Three or four days travel isn't bad, we could do that." Del mused.

"Ya," Charlie agreed, "next time we have a good supply of furs we will find that place across the Peace.

# Chapter 33
## THE MOOSE

It was May before the snow and ice melted and the streams and rivers were running freely again. Thoughts about the Hudson Bay Trading Post and the adventure of traveling further north to find it had plagued Del throughout the long winter months.

With the arrival of spring, Del was back to wandering again, wandering far and wide, looking over new countryside. Leaving the cabin early one morning, he told Charlie that he was going hunting. Charlie watched Del throw on his backpack and before Del picked up his rifle, Charlie knew he wouldn't be back for a day or two at the least.

It was late that same day when Del found himself near a river. He thought it would be a good place to make camp for the night. Putting his pack down, he rummaged through it until he found his fishing line and fishhooks. Pushing over some rocks bedded into the soft earth he found a couple of large worms for bait. The time of day must have been just right, for in no time at all he had caught a couple of fish, enough for his supper. He built up a good fire then set about cleaning out his fish. It took a little while because he had to clean off all the scales. Taking a small pan out of his camping supplies he was about to start frying his supper when an Indian walked out of the woods and down to the river. Del must have been concentrating very hard on his task of cooking because he never heard a sound when the Indian appeared.

The Indian said not a word to Del, just walked right past him to the river's edge. He moved downstream a ways not far from Del, built a fire and began fishing. While Del tended to his fish in the pan he watched the Indian bring out a good size fish. The Indian paid no mind to Del, but Del watched him with curiosity as he cleaned his fish. He cut the belly of the fish open and took out all the innards. Going to the river, he scooped up a little water and poured it on the dirt pushing it around to make thick mud. He rolled the fish in this mud and when it was completely covered, picked up the fish and placed it right into the coals of the fire.

Del had never seen such a thing. He continued to watch as the Indian left his fire and began to cut off branches of an evergreen tree. With a soft pile of the branches he made himself a bed. By then his fish was cooked. He pulled it out of the coals; the mud was baked hard and when he broke the mud off, all the scales came off with it. His fish was ready to eat for supper.

A word was never spoken between the two men as they camped at the same river's edge. Later, as Del settled down for the night with his blanket on the ground, he thought about what he had learned here. This man camping nearby didn't have a pan or any tools except the fish line and hook. He did have a blanket, a knife and a hatchet. It was hard to believe how little the Indian needed to survive. It was something he would never forget.

The next morning Del went through a big pine wood. Once on the other side, he found himself in a swampy area. He stopped tromping and looked around trying to get his bearings. Not far ahead he saw a great set of antlers. He could not see the animal but could see the antlers were very large. Standing very still, he patiently waited. Finally the antlers moved and he could see the head of a big moose feeding off the brush in the swamp. Slowly Del moved a little closer. Each time the moose picked his head up, Del would stop and stand still. When he thought he was close enough, he carefully brought up his rifle and with one shot, brought the big moose down.

He had a lot of meat to carry back to camp. Del picked up the end of one of the antlers and whistled low. The meat would be great to have back at the cabin, but those antlers would be a swell trophy. He wanted that great set of antlers; he couldn't leave it behind. There had to be a way to take them back. Working feverishly to cut off the antlers, he finally managed to break away most of the head, leaving the lower jaw. He had his antlers! But with a defeated sigh, he realized he was not going to be able to take those antlers back with him. They were just too big and heavy. He sat down to catch his breath. Discouraged, he leaned back with his hands stretched out behind him and rested. Now what? He couldn't just leave them here, not after all that work. Looking around he noticed a large pine tree with many low branches that would be easy to climb. He stood up, dragged the antlers to the tree, climbed up as far as he could go and looped a rope around the branch. Climbing back down he then tied the antlers to the rope and using the other end of the rope he hauled them up. Climbing back up the tree, he managed to get the antlers settled across a high branch where they wouldn't fall off. Here they would be safe until he could return to get them when he had nothing else to carry. He retrieved his rope and scurried back down the tree.

As Del walked toward the trapper's cabin, the moose meat weighed heavily in his backpack. He couldn't waste time since soon the wolves and coyotes would catch the scent of the meat he was carrying.

It took him another whole day to return to the cabin, marking his trail all the way. He hoped his markings would lead him back to retrieve the antlers, if he were to ever make another journey.

# Chapter 34
## HUDSON'S HOPE

Del was fix'n to cook a good meal of moose meat when Charlie came in from his trap line with a good catch. Charlie unloaded his catch and Del helped him clean and starch the furs. All the while they worked Charlie listened to Del ramble on about making a journey to search for the village of Hudson's Hope, the place the old miner told them they would find the trading post.

Taking his hat off, Charlie looked over at Del where he was stretching a beaver pelt. "Bloody hells, Del, you's really going to look for this place aren't you? Well, we might as well go together. It might be worth look'n fer."

Del was happy to hear it. "Alright! We have plenty of furs here to take. I think we can make the journey in a few days. We've heard tell a lot about Peace River, it will be grand to really see it. There is no way to miss the river if we travel due north and then go west. We will find Hudson's Hope sooner or later."

When Curley and Cowboy showed up later that same day, Del and Charlie told them their plans. But they didn't want anything to do with traipsing through the countryside not knowing for sure if they would even find the place. Besides, it was spring and the traps were doing good every day.

The next day, packhorses loaded with furs and camping supplies, Del and Charlie left their trapper's cabin and rode north. They found a path that wound about following a small creek. The path made it easier going; all the while they relied on their compass to make sure they were going due north. When the path faded the ride became slower as they made their way through brush and rough terrain. When they finally came to a flat, open space they set up camp for their first night out. Although daylight stretched a little longer into the afternoon now that spring had arrived, the darkness would soon overtake them as the cool night air set in. They tethered the horses and let them eat on the fresh grasses. After building a fire they cooked supper in a pot over the open flames and then brewed some coffee. Sitting on the ground with his back against his saddle, Del rested while drinking a mug of hot coffee. The stars began to appear one by one as the sky turned dark.

"The sky is clear of clouds tonight," he told Charlie. "It's a good night to sleep out in the open. I don't know how many miles we made today, but I think we did alright."

The night sounds surrounded them as Charlie picked up a long stick and stoked up the fire. "I feel like we are the only humans out here for miles and miles around. Hope you're right about finding that river by staying straight north," he said. "I sure hope the days and nights stay as dry as they are today. What's the name of this place we are searching for? I know you told me enough times."

"Hudson's Hope," Del said.

"Strange. Wonder why they gave it that name?"

"The old miner told us, didn't you listen to his story? I listened very close." Del replied. "It was a very old settlement, the miner said. Nobody knew for sure how it got its name. Some said it was because originally it was the location of the Hudson Bay's trading post which started over a hundred years ago. Others claimed it was named after a trapper named Hudson. The old miner told us that it's high up the Peace River. There is a settlement where the river first comes into view from the canyon of the Rocky Mountains and enters the plain country. It is the last trading post for Hudson Bay on the verge of the mountains."

"Ya, I remember that, Charlie said. "Peace River, the name has a nice sound to it, don't it? Like the land we travel, a place of solitude and calmness in the wilderness. Sometimes I think if we keep going we will find Alaska."

"I asked that miner about Peace River. He said it begins deep in the mountains far west where the great Finlay and Parsnip Rivers join together creating the Peace. The river runs east carving its way directly through the Rockies and north, eventually empting into the Artic Ocean," Del explained. "Sounds like a mighty big river to me."

It was during the next day they picked up an ancient trail. The trail was worn well and had been used by horses, trappers and Indians traveling on foot. The land turned from rolling hills to mountainous ridges and thickly wooded forests.

Following this trail for two days they emerged from a wood of cypress trees onto an open space; beneath ran the Peace River. On the opposite shore was a small settlement nestled among the wilderness.

"There she is!" Charlie said as they sat on their horses looking down over the edge of a ravine across the river to the sight of the small settlement. Waving high in the breeze they saw a bright red flag with the British Union Jack in one corner, the flag of the Hudson Bay Trading Company. Next to the flagpole was a large squared log building with a store attached and two small outhouses behind. A dozen or so cabins spread about making up the town.

Del looked up, moved his hat back as he grinned. "Yes sir, Mr. Johnson! We found it! We are here!"

The Peace River did not disappoint them. It was as big, strong and mighty as they imagined. The melting snow and ice of spring sent swollen streams rushing out of the many valleys of the mountains into the river, adding to its greatness as it majestically flowed with ease past them.

"Well," Del said, "Now that we've found the Peace, we've got to get across it. Let's make camp down there on the banks of the river."

They made camp for the night, not knowing what plan of action they would take to get across the river. Del had thoughts of making a raft but the river was very wide and it would be a long ways for the horses to swim. Early the next morning, they began searching up and down the river to find the best place for a crossing. They hadn't been out there too long when a large barge came into view slowly working its way down river from the west. The barge was loaded down with furs and pelts and was going to pass right by them toward a landing on the other side of the river.

Quickly they ran to the waters edge, waved their hats over their heads as they shouted and whistled. They were noticed and the barge stopped. Three men on board called out to them.

"We need to cross the river," Del shouted, "Can we get a ride?"

One of the men yelled back and said they would unload at the dock and come back for them. They cleaned up their campsite and waited with the horsesat the river's edge for the barge to return. True to the man's word the barge returned and brought them safely across the large river, horses and all.

They learned that the men with the barge had a trap line a few miles west of where they were. The current easily carried them downstream to the landing where the steamer would come and go from St. John, a town fifty miles to the east. Going back was a little harder moving up river, but they were empty by then and the waters were generally mild enough to navigate back to the shore near their cabin.

Besides the trading post, the town consisted of a post office, a hotel and a church, along with several cabins where the townsfolk lived. The spring of the year had brought out many other trappers to the trading post. The men were all dressed about alike with heavy greasy clothes that they had been wearing in the woods for some time. Among the trappers was a group of Indians. The place was noisy as the men all seemed to be having a good time. As Del and

Charlie walked inside, an older Indian was talking loudly and showing off something in his hand.

"What do you think it is?" He kept asking the group milling about. Several guesses came from the crowd, all wrong. The old Indian's eyes landed on Del and Charlie as they stood back against the wall. He maneuvered his way over to them. Holding up a tiny black dried up thing in Del's face, his voice boomed,

"Do you know what this is?"

As Del looked at it, he suddenly thought about the big beaver he had killed on the lake that was full of tiny unborn kits. He looked at the Indian and quietly said, "Well, yes, I believe I do."

Surprised the Indian said, "So what is it?"

Del replied, "I believe that is a baby beaver that was never born."

The old Indian put his arm down, slapped Del on the back exclaiming, "Smart man, smart man!"

With this all of the others laughed and seemed happy to finally find out what the big mystery was. Del and Charlie had a good time at Hudson's Hope. They listened to all the stories and added a few of their own. They heard many fishing and bear stories from the Indians. The Indians of this area were from the Beaver tribe. They were nomads with no fixed place to call home. They spent the summers hunting and fishing, and the winters trapping.

A few days later, their trading finished, the trappers with the barge were leaving and offered them a ride. They crossed back over the Peace River and followed their trail going south and east this time; a strong Chinook wind urged them along their way. Swiftly they rode. They had reached their destination, made good on their trade and seen the magnificence of the Peace River. They had journeyed on a road less traveled. On the other side of Hudson's Hope the mountains rose high. This country was where they now called home, where they worked and lived, surviving in an untamed land, deep into the Northwest Provinces of Canada. This was a place were men had traveled before, but few had stayed.

# Chapter 35
## A Goose Hunt

A small lake was not far from the main trapper's cabin. Del was walking through high willow brush, tangled vines, and dead wood when he found a swarm of mosquitoes. It was rough going. He should have gone a different way around all this mess, but it would have taken him longer to get to the water. Finally, he broke free and came to the shore. The shimmering water gleamed bright gold reflecting off the sun as it rose over the trees. The air smelled of wet wood, moss and soggy ground.

Just as he arrived at the water's edge a large goose flew up out of the lake. Wings flapping and loudly honking, the bird was not close enough to get in a good shot. Suddenly, from somewhere else on the lakeshore, a shot rang out. Del watched as the goose flew a ways, came closer to him, then dropped into the water. Del reacted quickly and ran along the shore until he could see the fallen goose. Nearby, a dead tree had fallen over into the water. It looked dry and had been there a long time, but he knew it would not be long enough to reach the goose floating in the lake. Running back inland a bit he searched the dead wood lying about and found a long branch on the ground. Carefully he walked out onto the fallen tree to the very end. The dead goose was floating in the water very near but not quite close enough to reach. Hanging onto the branch he laid down on the tree and moved his body out as far as he could without falling off. He reached out with his arm, and with the stick outstretched he was able to reach the bird and pull it in. Carrying the goose back into the woods he carefully hung it up in a tree and continued on his way.

Charlie, Curley and Cowboy had all spread out in different directions during this hunting expedition. When Dell got back to their meeting point the others were already there. None of them had any luck. There would be no duck or goose for supper tonight.

"I shot at a big goose," Curley said. "I didn't think I'd hit him but had to try. I saw him fly up and I shot but it kept flying and I didn't see him again."

"Ya, I heard the shot." Del said not looking at him, keeping his eyes on their path. Charlie and Cowboy agreed they had heard the shot too and thought for sure someone would have a big goose.

Curley stopped at a thicket near the water. "That goose flew up out of this area. I'll bet there's a nest in there." They all started searching; pulling back brush close to the shore. There, sure enough, was a nest with eggs.

"Hey hey hey!" Curley shouted, "We won't have goose but we sure will have some fresh eggs!"

The men where excited. Fresh eggs would be a real treat. Not as good as fresh roasted goose, but a treat just the same. They went a little further down the path and Del stopped.

"I'll be right back." He announced. Without another word he left them and walked back to the tree where he had left the goose. Coming back out he held the bird up high for the other fellas to see.

Surprised, Charlie, Curley and Cowboy stared at him in disbelief.

"We'll have a good feast tonight." Del said. "Here's your goose!"

# Chapter 36
## SUMMER COMES AGAIN

As summer arrived, once again the trapping business slowed. Charlie and the others were off checking the lines and Del found he was alone at the main cabin. A warm breeze flowed through the open door. Del listened to the sounds of a nice summer day as he drank his morning coffee. Blaze whinnied as he paced inside the pen. Walking out to check on his horse, Del called and talked to him as he began to brush him down.

"You are as restless as I am, aren't you, boy. Well, maybe it's time to go for a small journey. We'll go see Mark Debral and see if I've got any mail. How's that sound?"

Blaze nickered as if to answer. They were soon on their way. Del packed enough grub and gear to be out a few days, but if he headed straight for Mark Debral's place, he could be there in a few hours.

Mark was happy to see him, as usual, and sure enough, just as he had hoped, a few letters were waiting for him. One from his mother, one from his sister Luella and one was postmarked Burns Lake, BC from Gaylord Stearns.

Del didn't open his letters right away; he was busy talking with Mark. The front door was wide open letting in the air and sunshine. Suddenly, the two men heard a horse approaching. Del was surprised to see the young man who was walking through the open door was one of the two brothers he had helped to cross the river.

Del shook his hand. "Paul Jackson, I didn't think I would see you again"

"Hey, Del," Paul replied, "You still around this area?"

"We've got a trap line not far from here." Del said. "Charlie and I found a couple other guys and went into partnership with them. Did you make it to your homestead okay?"

"We did: we've got a good cabin built and a nice garden growing now." Paul replied as he nodded his head while thinking back to that trip. "It was twenty miles from here across that mountain, a rough trip that took us twenty-two days. Halfway we met some Indians that were out hunting. They had just killed a moose and they gave us some of the meat. That sure helped a lot." As an afterthought Paul added, "And that five dollars that Charlie gave us really helped a lot, too."

Del blinked at the words, "It's good to know you are all okay." He said.

Del felt a little foolish thinking about Charlie giving them money. He could have just as well given them some money, too, but the thought never occurred to him. That was generous of Charlie; he just wished he could have been as thoughtful. Well, it was too late now.

The three men shared some coffee and biscuits and then Paul picked up his supplies and wanted to start back for home before it got too late. Del had no thoughts of going back that day; tomorrow would be better. After Paul left, Mark was busy taking care of the recent furs that Paul had brought in and Del sat down and pulled out his letters from home.

Mother's letter was full of home and news about his brothers and their families. Clint and Homer were the only ones at home now; Homer was still just a young boy. Emery was in the Army fighting over in Europe. Ozzie and Alice have three children now, and Herb and Maysie are parents of five. The families were growing fast. Mother enjoys their new home in Knapps Station and Pa and the boys had just finished building a new barn. They were getting to know their new neighbors. Abe and Nellie Nichols were an especially nice family and had become good friends. Luella's letter was a surprise and it was good to hear from her. She and her husband, Zene, bought a home in Massena and their two little boys, Wayne and Ernie, were keeping her busy. The boys were just babies the last time that Del had seen them. She also had news and gossip about their brothers and sister, Mina, and the goings on in their lives. Things that mother would never tell him.

Del was most curious to find out what the letter from Stearns was all about. He had saved it to read last.

*Dear Del,*

*Received your letter here last week and Bessie and I are both happy to hear you are surviving and doing well up there in the wild country.*

*I just came back from the trap line and did okay. I have a good trap line and the older boys, Harry and Ralph, help out with it. Nice to have my boys working with me. We did a little gold prospecting, too, this spring. We didn't find much this time. There is still gold in those mountain streams; one of these days I'll strike it rich, yet.*

*The hardware store has been busy. The business is good and our town is growing with new people moving in all the time. The tent town has been replaced with homes and new streets.*

*I've got a fellow interested in buying out the hardware store. I'll have to say this type of business is really not for me. My bookkeeping is not the best. I'm looking at buying a little ranch out in the country not far off from Burns Lake. And I have this idea of raising beavers. I think it can be done and be done well. The boys are big enough to work on the ranch and it will give all the kids more room to run about.*

*Bessie is well and cheerful as ever, busy as Fred and Gaylord Joseph are still little. Grace is a big help for her mother.*

*Maybe one of these days you can make it over here to Burns Lake for a visit. Would be good to see you. You can find us, just check out a good map and you will find us okay. There are roads now, better than the trails through the bush like when we first arrived and we have the best fishing anywhere around.*

*You take care and be careful of the bears in that country. Write again soon. As always, your friend,*
*R G Stearns*


Del folded the letter and thought about Gaylord raising wild beaver and he chuckled to himself. He always was one for chasing after his pot of gold. Seemed like he had many dreams and schemes and they never turned out. Maybe this ranch would be a good success. Del hoped so for his dear friend.

Del bought some paper and envelopes and by the end of the day he had written back to Gaylord, Luella and his mother. He assured Mother that all was well and he was warm and well fed. The thoughts of home and longing to see the families that were changing so much were very strong on his mind. He began to think about his life in this wilderness. What he would do with his life ahead of him had never clearly been thought out. He was making good money and saving plenty. But saving for what? He could travel back home someday and have enough to start over. Enough to manage very well. But, going back home, when? No, he decided as he sat there holding his letters, he was not ready to return just yet.

On his way back to the trapper's cabin, Del wanted to do some hunting. Summer trapping was slow and they needed meat. He moved off the trail to the north and up a mountain. Once over the mountaintop he could see around the country and easily look it over. The land seemed to be mostly rocky ledges and rugged country. He did get a glimpse of an elk and her calf, but she was gone before he could get a shot at her. As he scanned the open slopes and valleys, he saw a black bear not far off to his right. The bear was on the run toward another hill. Watching the bear run toward the right side of the hill, Del decided to go to the left and meet the bear on the other side. As Del came around the hill, he slowed and dropped down off Blaze. With his rifle ready, he carefully walked ahead expecting to meet that bear. Nothing was there. Looking around he could see the bear running down the hill toward a big open valley. By this time he was quite a distance away. Del carefully took aim and fired. The bear stopped, stood up on his hind legs, dropped down and started running again. Blood was running down the bear's front leg so he knew for sure he had hit him. Swiftly, Del ran after him as the bear headed down into the big valley. Stopping again, he fired a second time and this time the bear dropped. Dell watched as the bear rolled down the hill and was stopped by a big rock.

Del ran back up the hill to retrieve Blaze and rode down to where the bear lay. Swiftly, he skinned out the bear to keep the hide and took all the meat that he could pack into the saddlebags. This huge hide would be great to have.

When Del finished he sat down to rest. It had been a long day; he was tired and he still had to get down off that mountain. He rode Blaze for a short ways down to the valley and made camp along a mountain stream where he found plenty of dead wood to build a fire away from the wind. He would camp out one more night. The next day would be soon enough to find his way back to the main camp.

# Chapter 37

## THE STALKER

I t happened that summer, Curly and Cowboy decided to leave. They had enough of living on the trap line and were not looking forward to another winter. The money they had made was even more than they had hoped for and now they wanted to sell out their share to Del and Charlie. Del was surprised at their decision but it didn't bother him much; he had never taken a big liking to them anyway. He and Charlie would get along without them. Del had put up the biggest share in the beginning, so they bought out what was owed of Curly and Cowboy's shares and said their goodbyes, wishing them well.

Firewood needed to be cut and stacked for all of the cabins, as well as the main cabin, and repairs made. With just the two of them now, the work would take longer. Summer season was a few short months and the first weeks had passed rainy and cool.

The first morning that promised a decent day they took the pack horses and rode the trail to Ed Finney's trading post. As they traveled, Dell began to look forward to a big meal, maybe even chicken and dumplings, and a big piece of pie, any kind of pie. They always ate well at the cabin but his own cooking was getting tiresome. There were lots of people at the little post. A few more cabins and homes had been added since their last visit, making the post more of a village. Del enjoyed the commotion and watching the different types of people working and moving about. Here they found news of the outside world they had been wondering about. The Great War in Europe was still going on. They were lucky, today's menu had chicken and dumplings and fresh berry pie. The day passed quickly making their stay at Ed Finney's seem short. Loaded up with all the supplies they needed, they headed back to the cabin before daylight faded away.

Summer had quite vanished by the time they finished with all of the little cabins and September had arrived. Calmness fell over the land and an occasional white frost in the mornings gave warning of the winter to come. Del was ready to go wandering again and do some hunting. This time it wasn't hard to talk Charlie into going with him.

They traveled for a day, crossed the west branch of the Pine River and set up camp at the base of a mountain. The next morning Del and Charlie split up as they worked their way up the mountain. Hopefully, one of them would scare up some game into the sights of the other. The going was pretty rough on the pine tree covered slope and it wasn't long before Del lost track of Charlie.

While he was working around house-sized boulders, he started to get a feeling of foreboding. The forest was absolutely quiet, even the birds had fallen silent. Del was not superstitious but the feeling grew stronger as he continued. Briefly he flirted with the idea that the mountain was haunted, but he quickly cast that idea aside. Still, something felt wrong and he just could not shake it. He came across a faint game trail and started following it down a steep ravine. The trail led to an almost vertical drop into a deep gully. Del stopped by a tree looking out over the gorge and considered turning back. This wild country was no place to break a leg while following a game trail that might only be used by mountain goats. As he stood by the tree surveying the place, he slowly came to the realization that the feeling he had was one of being watched, maybe even stalked. The hunter had become the hunted. He stood stock still, straining his ears to hear anything out of the ordinary. Suddenly, even though he had not heard anything, he knew that he was not alone. The hair on the back of his neck stood up. Something was very close. On impulse Del whirled around and found himself face-to-face with a huge grizzly bear. Del was sure the bear had him in mind for lunch. In that same split second of realization, Del knew he had to act fast. His rifle flew up toward the bear as if it had a mind of its own. No time to put the rifle to his shoulder and aim, just point and pull the trigger. The gun roared at the same time the bear pounced. Del jumped to the side barely being missed by the huge bulk, its pungent musky odor mixing with the smell of gun smoke. The great beast lunged to the spot Del had been standing and fell down stone dead. The bullet had miraculously found its way straight to the animal's heart. Del wiped the sweat from his brow with a shaking hand and let out a long sigh.

"I don't think I could ever make a shot like that again", he muttered to himself. Just to be sure, he racked another shell into the chamber of the gun and put a bullet into the bear's brain.

Charlie wasn't far away and when he heard the rifle shots he found his way to Del and the bear. Jumping off his horse, his Irish accent came out strong in his excitement.

"Look at this beast! I would never have expected to see a grizzly this size when I heard your shot. Any kind of animal went through my head, but not this!"

Del was still in shock as he sat down on a nearby boulder, relief slowly flowing through him. "This grizzly almost had me for lunch. He snuck up on me so close I could almost feel his breath down my neck!"

Their hunt was done. They would have all the meat they could possibly carry and Del really wanted the hide. This one would certainly be worth something. They went to work and skinned the grizzly. They were able to carry back the best cuts of the bear meat to load into the horses' saddlebags. The horses put up a fuss, their ears back and eyes wild with fright as the men first approached. The smell of the bear sent them into a panic. Del kept softly talking to Blaze as he slowly walked closer. Eventually the horse calmed letting Del touch him, reassuring no danger. Once Blaze calmed down the other horses quieted too.

They traveled toward home for as long as they could that day. As it started to get dark they found a sheltered area and made camp for the night. Afraid that the smell of the blood and bear meat would attract some wolves or coyotes, they kept the campfire well stocked up for the whole night.

When they got back to the cabin, the first thing they did was to store most of the meat into their tree cache. There it would be safe and keep well with the cold weather. They then tended their horses and brought in enough wood for the fire. "The bear had to have been an old geezer to have been as big as he was," Del thought, so he put some of the meat into a big kettle with water, salt and pepper slowly cooking it for a few hours. While the meat cooked he and Charlie went to work outside to clean the skin of the bear, stretching it and letting it dry. Returning to the now warm and cozy cabin, the smell of the simmering bear meat filled their senses making them hungry. Charlie cooked a few apples picked from a wild apple tree he had found on the way home. Del made biscuits and tea and their meal was soon ready. They were so hungry by this time that anything would have tasted good. Finishing the last of the meat in the pan, both agreed they would rather have had venison or even beef.

Silently, the first snow of the season began to fall. Morning would be the beginning of one more long, cold and desolate winter on the trap line.

# Chapter 38
## THE LAST WINTER

S pring was close at hand and an early thaw had allowed Del and Charlie to take the horses out and make a trip to Mark Debral's. Del had been eager to look for mail and the nice weather made him restless.

While warming themselves by the woodstove, Mark greeted them with all the news he had learned from his latest trip out to the Peace River to pick up supplies and mail from the boat. It was a relief to hear the great news that the war had ended; an armistice had been signed in November. This was several months ago and the troops were on their way home. Del took his single letter from home and sat by the window where the bright sunlight shone through.

*Dear son,*

*I have sad news to tell you. Although it is not good news, it could be worse. We have heard from Emery. He was seriously wounded some time ago and is now in a hospital in New York City. His leg is badly hurt and he might never walk again. We thank God he is alive and pray that he will soon be home, although he says the doctor tells him it could be several months before he will be ready to leave. The terrible war is over and the soldiers are coming home from overseas.*

*It has been some time since we have heard from you and I'm sure the winter has been long and cold for you. It has been very cold here as well but lately the weather has been mild. It is Sunday afternoon, many of the local children are skating on the brook and I walked to church this morning. Yesterday I finished sewing new curtains for the downstairs kitchen and front room. It is nice to have Mahoney's store nearby where I can buy cloth, threads and almost anything else I need. Pa spends a lot of time there talking with the men as they come and go passing the cold days away.*

*Pa has rented out the family farm. He held a big auction and sold off many of his mules, but he was not ready to sell off all of his mares and mules so he made an agreement to leave some of them there to be taken care of by the renters. None of the boys wanted to take over the old family farm as Herb and Maisie have their own place and Ozzie and Alice are all settled in their home close by us in Knapps. Clint and Lena are living on Croil's Island where Lena teaches school and Homer is still just a boy living at home with us. Here at our new place Pa has kept his favorite set of bays and is still raising foxhounds.*

*I hope you are safe and well. Please write soon. I pray for you each night.*

*Love, Mother*

"Imagine that!" Del said quietly. He looked at his two friends in exasperation. "The war is over, but as luck would have it, not before my brother Emery got wounded." He turned his letter over and read it again. "It says Emery is seriously hurt, he has been sent to a hospital in New York City and he might never walk again. That's all! Mother doesn't say what happened, how he got hurt or when."

Worried, he crossed his arms and leaned back in his chair tipping it back on two legs. The words 'might never walk again', burned into his mind. He couldn't picture Emery living that way.

Mark got up and poured coffee into tin mugs and brought one to each of them.

"That's rotten luck if ever there was any", he said to Del as he handed him one of the cups. "But a lot of our boys have died over there and your brother is still alive."

"That's right," Charlie agreed, "and your ma said he might not walk again. Sounds like that's not a sure thing."

Del's friends were trying to be encouraging and it helped relieve the worry.

Del, lost in thought, didn't say anything for several minutes. With a large sigh, he set his cup down on the floor beside his chair, shaking his head slightly he replied:

"I can't help but think it could have been so different. If Emery had stayed on the prairie with me, we could've had us quite a good farm by now. He never would have been in the army and sent overseas."

Charlie watched Del stand up and pace about the room. Del heard him talking but wasn't really listening. Finally he sat back down and asked Charlie, "What did you say? I wasn't paying attention."

"Del, I said you never would still be there! Think about it. If you had stayed on that homestead both of you might have been over there fighting that war. Besides, things have a way of working out. You just have to wait and see."

Del looked at his good friend and said, "The waiting is what's bad. I won't know for weeks, maybe months."

Del took time to write a letter back to his mother and wondered how long it would be before she would even get it. For the first time in a long time he wished he were home. He had a strong need to be among his family and know what was happening, not just to Emery but to all of them.

Del was unusually silent on the trip back to the cabin. For many days afterwards he worked mechanically, eating, sleeping, working the days away but it wasn't making them pass any faster. Finally an evening came when he opened up his thoughts to Charlie. Outside the wind blew strong driving a forceful spring rain against the cabin. Del was sitting, whittling at a piece of wood, a lantern on the table giving out the only light.

"I think its time for me to take a trip home, Charlie. When summer comes; it's been nine years." Sitting back he looked over at Charlie, "I'm not sure I'll be back."

Charlie was putting away the tobacco tin after filling his pipe. He turned and sat in one of the crude chairs beside the fire. Looking thoughtfully at Del he nodded his head, "Yup, I kinda thought this was coming. Ya know, I've been in one place too long anyway; I need to move on, too. I've been thinking of heading farther east. Maybe I'll even find a woman to settle down with."

"You could never find a woman to put up with you for long!" Del laughed and it broke the mood.

A good woman, a home and a family, it sounded good. It was the life Del had been brought up with, the life he ran away from. Time had a way of changing ideas and thoughts. He was getting no younger and maybe before he found himself to be an old man he should try to make this kind of life for himself, too.

As the squall outside carried on, the anxiety inside Del began to ease and for the first time in a long time, he comfortably slept well through the night. The decision had been made; Del had made up his mind once and for all to go home. As usual, once he made a decision he didn't look back, only forward. There was no sense in leaving now; it would be better to wait until summer. They could make more money working the rest of the season on the trap line and offer it for sale in the summer. Besides, traveling would be much better in nice weather.

Summer came early that year. Del and Charlie started to get ready for their trip east. Their life of trappers in the Northwest Territory was now over; new horizons lay ahead of them.

Ed Finney readily agreed to buy the trap line himself. More people were moving into the area and men where always looking for a good trap line. After all the furs he had seen come into his trading post, he knew it was a good investment. Ed had seen many trappers come and go. Del and Charlie would be far from the last to cross his path.

With the main cabin cleaned out Del and Charlie rode their saddle horses and lead one packhorse each to carry all their worldly possessions.

Before leaving they needed to make one more stop at Mark Debral's. Mark gave them extra supplies needed to prepare for the long trip and didn't charge them anything. He was sorry to see them g,o but he knew these young men needed to move on and make a life for themselves, not secluded here in the wilderness for the rest of their lives.

"You're going home Del, that's a good thing for you. You've been away long enough. Don't try to spend your life here and end up like me." His laugh was jolly as he continued, "If you stayed here, before you know it you would be old and grumpy." He watched them ride out of sight disappearing among the trees as the path wound away from the river into the forest.

Riding east and south, Del and Charlie were several days into their journey to Edmonton, their final destination before parting ways, when they could see a river stretching out in the horizon. They came to the river the same time as a group of about twenty men arrived from the other side. Del and Charlie dismounted as they watched the men swim their horses across. As the men came to shore, they also got off their horses to talk to the two travelers. The two explained to the men that they were on their way to Edmonton and were told they had a few days travel yet ahead of them.

"You are trappers coming out of that wild land, are you? Where was your trap line?" one of the men asked.

Turning Blaze about Del sat still for a moment looking back over the land. A large hawk soared overhead searching for an easy prey in the open grassland. With the bright sun now high in the sky they had been traveling several hours since breaking camp that morning. A warm breeze gave relief from the scorching heat. Forested hills made a scraggly background stretching out across the landscape of the Peace River country. They were now into Alberta. British Columbia stretched behind them. One last look, the destination he had claimed; as far west as he could travel. A different world, he thought to himself, a whole different world indeed. It had been the life of a different person than the boy who had first wandered west nine years before. He had worked ranches in Montana, homesteaded on the prairie, and been a mountain man living off the land, among the wild and unknown. Now, he was going home.

Del turned back toward the traveler. "Peace River country, east of the Pine", he replied, "It's a big place over there."

"Well, we are on our way to somewhere in that wilderness of British

Columbia to claim homesteads. We're just back from the war, every one of us, and the government has granted us some land for homesteading."

The group of men moved on as Del and Charlie watched them go after wishing them good luck. As a result of the homesteads allotted to veterans for soldier settlements after World War I, the remote villages and places of British Columbia that Del had traveled would soon grow and flourish.

Edmonton was a busy city. Streets lined with boardwalks and gas lamps to light up the night. Many automobiles ran up and down the streets among a few horse and buggies. They found a hotel to stay for a night, a warm bath and good meal. Del felt refreshed after a good night's sleep in a real bed. Clean-shaven and wearing a set of clean clothes he set out to sell his horses.

"I'll need to buy my ticket and find out when the train leaves," he told Charlie. Charlie, as well, had cleaned up and looked a site younger with no whiskers and new clothes on. Together they found some stables where Del sold his two horses. A tight feeling wrapped its way around Del's chest as he gave an affectionate pat to Blaze. Suddenly his throat hurt as he tried to speak. Blaze had been a true and faithful friend for a long time. "Take good care of this one." He said as he shook hands with the stable hand and he turned and walked away.

"Massena, New York", he told the ticket master at the train station. Looking diligently through his book the gray haired, slightly bald man said, "I have no such place on my books". Del was puzzled; had he been gone so long that the railroad station in Massena no longer existed? "Try Norwood, New York," Del said after trying to think quickly of what other town close by had a train station. Norwood was one of the major train depots in St. Lawrence County at that time.

"I do have a station at Norwood, New York," the old man replied.

"Well, Norwood will do and is probably better anyway," Del said, somewhat relieved that he could still get home. The train would leave early the next morning.

Charlie was already in the lobby when Del arrived to check out.

"Here is where we part ways, my friend." Del again felt the band of tightness around his chest, knowing he would most likely never see Charlie again. Charlie had not yet decided his next destination and planned to stay at the hotel for a time.

"May the wind always be at your back, Del", Charlie said as the two men shook hands for the last time. "Thanks, Charlie, good luck to you." Del felt his friend's hand tighten the grip. He let out a big sigh and turned to walk to the train depot. Del had many friends along his journey since he first traveled west, but Charlie would remain long in his memory.

Mountains, valleys and fields of green lush woodlands passed by the train window as the train traveled through the northeast on the way to northern New York. The ride had been very long by the time Del arrived in the village of Norwood. The station was busy with people coming and going. Many were waiting to board and others were there to meet travelers. Mechanic Street, Norwood was a narrow street leading out to Main with many little shops on both sides of the street.

"When does the train leave for Knapps Station?" He asked.

"In just about an hour; Knapps will be our first stop when we leave here."

Perfect, thought Del. He hadn't written his folks as to when he would arrive; nobody was waiting for him.

It didn't take long to go the six miles from Norwood to North Stockholm, a hamlet built up around the railroad depot and flourishing along the shores of Plumbbrook. Officially named North Stockholm, it was commonly known as Knapps Station after Moses Knapp, a man who owned property there and ran the depot many years ago. As the train rolled up to the station where it stopped twice a day, the whistle blew loud and long announcing its arrival.

The little station wasn't quite as busy as Norwood. Del picked up his bags and walked to the street, a dusty dirt road lined with homes, big elms and maples. He had never been to his folks' new home, but Mother had written in her letters that it was across the road from where the milk factory was being rebuilt, and close to Ozzie and Alice.

From the station he could see a blacksmith shop next to the brook, and not far down the road among a few houses, a small shop on the right, a large store was on the left and the milk factory. Children ran, laughed and played as dust flew up from a horse drawn wagon going to the train station. A few men in the store watched him with curiosity as did Leora Nichols, a young lady inside the small shop. To them he was a handsome stranger who looked slightly familiar. Leora watched him walk to the Baxter home thinking, "the prodigal son they often talked about has long last arrived home." Little did she know at the time that she was looking at her destiny, the man with whom she would spend the rest of her life.

A large maple shaded freshly cut grass on the front lawn of the new house. A garden bordering the carriage barn boasted the beginnings of many fresh vegetables. Clothes on a line waved in the summer breeze. A wooden pail waited beside the iron pump at the well. When two fox hounds ran barking from the open door of the barn, Del knew he was at the right house. Laban Baxter emerged from the barn to see what all the barking was about. With hands on hips he watched Del walk down the driveway.

"I see you're still raising those fox hounds", Del said with a chuckle in his voice as he sat his bags down on the open porch of the house.

"And the best in the county they are too!" Pa exclaimed.

Mother came out on the porch drying her hands on her apron letting the wooden screen door slam behind her. Wisps of white hair pulled free from her usually neat bun, framing her plump face, red and clammy from the heat. "Del!" she cried. "Oh my goodness, it's Del." Hurrying down the steps, she embraced Del and, with a hankie retrieved from her apron pocket, wiped the tears from her eyes.

"So, are you here for just a visit or is this for good?" Pa asked.

"No, not a visit," Del said shaking his head. "I'm home for good."

The dogs quieted their barking as Mother urged Del into the house. "You must be starved; I've got coffee on the stove and just finished baking a cake. Come and sit and tell us all about where you have been. You must have some good stories to tell."

Del laughed out loud. His heart was light, he was happy to be home and, he had lots of stories to tell.

# *Afterward*

Once Del was settled in back home it didn't take him long to meet, fall in love with and marry Leora Nichols. Finally he had found happiness and contentment with a home, a good woman and children to pass his days with. It was not to last long however. Leora gave birth to their eighth child and shortly after both she and the baby died of pneumonia. Del was left to raise seven children alone, and that's exactly what he did. He never remarried, but instead devoted his life to his family He was a kind, soft-spoken man, a true 'gentleman' in every sense of the word.

In 1961, with his daughter, Dorothy, he made his last trip west to revisit the land of his prairie homestead in Alberta. To his surprise he found that, although moved to a different location, the house he built was still standing and being lived in by a young family. The owner of the property was happy to meet him. He told Del that he often thought about the old timers who settled there as he rode horseback around the land and found remnants of original homestead buildings, but he never thought he would ever get to meet one of them. Together they drove out to the location of Del's original homestead buildings. The only thing he found there was the well that he had dug almost fifty years before.

Del passed away in 1986 just six months short of his 100th birthday. Those of us here today can only imagine the magnificent wonders he saw and experienced in those 100 years! He left behind a close-knit family to carry on his legacy. His adventurous spirit, complete devotion to family and friends, and his yen for knowledge and new experiences will live on in the generations of his family that follow. To be remembered as a hardworking, proud and adventurous soul is a wonderful thing; for that is, indeed, the true pioneer spirit.

Del would relive his life out west and share his stories time and time again throughout many years to come. His adventures became stories for his children, grandchildren and great-grandchildren to grow up with. And so to preserve this time in his life we have written this book for the future generations of Delbert Baxter's family.

At the time of this writing Del's descendents total 142+. The family members are scattered around the world, living in several different states from the east coast to the west coast, and from the north to the south, and also in three other countries besides the US.

## More about Emery Baxter:

Emery never did return to his homestead on the prairie. Eventually, he joined the Army and during his enlistment took up boxing, becoming the champ of his unit. Emery carried his fearless attitude with him onto the battlefields of World War I where he became a hero and was awarded the Silver Star for bravery, the third highest Medal of Honor in the United States. Severely wounded, he spent many months recuperating in a hospital in New York City. Although fully recovered, he walked with a limp for the rest of his life, ending his boxing career. Often, Emery would talk about the desire to go back to Alberta, but he never was able to return and lick ole Johnson.

## More about Clint Baxter

Through out his lifetime Clint carried fond memories of his days spent on the prairie homestead with Del. He did travel around the country somewhat, but he spent the majority of his life near the Baxter family farm. He married Lena Gaines, a young school teacher, and together they raised eight children. He built a home and set up a saw mill in what is now known as Baxterville in St. Lawrence County. Like many men of his family, he made his living from working in the woods, logging and operating his saw mill.

## More about Ruben Gaylord and Bessie Stearns:

Gaylord and Bessie did build their hardware store but later moved their family to a ranch outside of town and spent the remaining years of their life in the area of Burns Lake, British Columbia. Gaylord passed away in 1944 and Bessie followed in 1956. Many letters passed between Del and the Stearns family throughout all of those years, but sadly, they were never to meet again.

# List of References

Peace River Chronicles
Selected and Edited by Gordon E. bowes
Prescott Publishing Company, 1963

Johnny Chinook Tall Tales and True From The Canadian West
By Robert Gard, Published 1945 by Longmans, Green & Company
Stories reprinted with the permission of the Estate of Robert E. Gard.

Glenbow Museum
130-9 Avenue S.E.
Calgary, AB Canada T2G0P3

Alberta Folklore and Local History
University of Alberta Librairies
http://folklore.library.ualberta.ca

Dorothy Baxter Arquette was born on a farm in Knapps Station, New York, the third of eight children. She has been married for sixty-eight years to Gordon Arquette. She is the author of the memoir *Thoughts of Long Ago*.

Judy Arquette Brassard was born to Dorothy and Gordon Arquette, the third of four children. She has published several short stories and poems in *The Storyteller, The Purple Pen, Flair,* and *The St. Lawrence County Historical Society Quarterly*. She and her husband, Michael, live in Hannawa Falls, New York.